THE END OF THE
CHINESE 'MIDDLE AGES'

*Essays in Mid-Tang
Literary Culture*

THE END OF THE
CHINESE 'MIDDLE AGES'

*Essays in Mid-Tang
Literary Culture*

Stephen Owen

Stanford University Press
Stanford, California

Stanford University Press
Stanford, California
© 1996 by the Board of Trustees of the
Leland Stanford Junior University

Printed in the United States of America

CIP data appear at the end of the book

Stanford University Press publications are
distributed exclusively by Stanford University Press
within the United States, Canada, Mexico, and Central America; they are distributed exclusively by Cambridge University
Press throughout the rest of the world.

❖

Acknowledgments

Versions of the following translations are reprinted, with permission, from Stephen Owen, *An Anthology of Chinese Literature: Beginnings to 1911*, published by W. W. Norton & Company, 1996.

Bai Juyi, "Choosing a Dwelling Place in Luoyang," "Eating Bamboo Shoots," "Reciting Poems Alone in the Mountains," "What Came to Mind When Chanting My Poems"

"Huo Xiaoyu's Story"

Li He, "Don't Go out the Gate," "A Long Song Follows a Short Song"

Liu Zongyuan, "An Account of Little Stone Ramparts Mountain," "An Account of the Small Hill West of Gumu Pond," "Theory of Heaven"

Meng Jiao, "Tormented"

Wang Han, " "Liangzhou Lyric"

Wang Wei, "Hollow by Meng's Walls"

"Yingying's Story"

Contents

THE END OF THE
CHINESE 'MIDDLE AGES'

Essays in Mid-Tang
Literary Culture

❖

Introduction

These essays come fifteen years after my last volume on the
history of Tang poetry, which treated the High Tang. During
the interval I have often been asked if I planned to continue
my works on Early Tang and High Tang poetry with a volume
on Mid-Tang poetry. The essays in the present volume are a
partial response to the impossibility of writing such a history
of Mid-Tang poetry.

The present essays are literary historical, but they do not,
in themselves, constitute a literary history. Rather than describing a process of change or giving a comprehensive account of major and minor writers, they follow an interrelated
set of issues through a variety of texts and genres. By their
nature these particular issues strongly suggest close connec-
tions to larger areas of cultural, and perhaps social, history.
On one level the texts discussed are themselves a part of
cultural history: the public account of acquisition and ownership, the wittily hyperbolic interpretation of the miniature
garden, and the discussion of romantic intrigues are acts of
social display in their own right, and the values they embody
must to some degree be assumed in the audience in which
these texts circulated. On another level, however, the ways in
which these discursive phenomena relate to more concrete
social practices—for example, patterns of landownership, garden construction, and concubinage—lie beyond the scope of
these essays.

A "history of Mid-Tang poetry" is inappropriate because

poetry in this period, dating roughly from 791 to 825, is less susceptible to separate generic treatment than the poetry of the Early Tang or High Tang. In style, in topics, and in norms of treatment, the poetry of the Mid-Tang is much more varied than that of the High Tang, and the ways in which the scope of poetry broadened and changed were closely tied to changes in other discursive forms. Poetry, classical tales, and nonfictional prose share common concerns in a way that occurs less frequently in the Early and High Tang. It was perhaps an intuition of this aspect of Mid-Tang poetry that led many influential critics from the thirteenth century on to condemn the poetry of this period as somehow less "poetic" than that of the High Tang. But the very breadth of Mid-Tang poetry, its movement beyond the limitations of earlier poetry, can also be its strength.

Modern literary theory alternates between asserting an economy of genres (that each discursive form is privileged to do things that other forms cannot) and asserting the shared historical basis for all forms of cultural representation within a given period. The former moment asserts that poetry or the novel or drama is somehow special, that it is primarily engaged in exploring its own generic possibilities and responding to its own generic history. The latter sees all contemporary discursive forms as sharing some common historical determination that transcends genre.[1]

Literary theory tends to ask for some decision between these opposed possibilities, or for an attempt to reconcile them. The alternatives are understood as "approaches" rather than historical distinctions that might exist in the material approached. In contrast, a historical point of view may say: "Sometimes more the one; sometimes more the other." During some periods there is, on balance, a strong economy of genre; this was largely true of the Early Tang and High Tang, and

---

[1] Bakhtin's claims about the novel, made in a context when similar claims were being made about the exclusive distinction of poetry, are a good example of the former moment. "New Historicism" and the so-called historical turn in cultural studies can represent the latter.

thus a "history of poetry" is possible. Mid-Tang poetry, however, broke away from the focus and restriction of genre. The concerns that so profoundly changed poetry in the Mid-Tang are found throughout Mid-Tang writing, and its history is no longer poetry's history alone.

The first of the essays, "Singularity and Possession," considers Mid-Tang representations of identity as an exclusion of or by others. At the level of individual identity, such singularity may appear as an assertion of superiority over others, but it may also be an alienation that brings rejection by others. In writing, singularity reveals itself as a unique and identifiable style that may be appropriated by others but always remains identified with the individual writer. In the famous "Letter in Reply to Li Yi," Han Yu likewise conceptualizes the process by which he perfected his prose as one of excluding elements that belong to (or please) others. Singularity is articulated in the same way at the level of corporate identities, as in the literary group that distinguishes itself from the larger community of writers, and, for Han Yu, in a vision of Chinese culture from which foreign elements (Buddhism) have been excluded. This version of singularity is formally identical to a new discourse of ownership, represented as the exclusion of others from access or possession.

The next essay, "Reading the Landscape," addresses different ways of representing landscapes, showing the ways in which the underlying order of nature has become a problem in the Mid-Tang. On the one side are texts that articulate and comment on the strict order of nature; such landscapes are architectonic to a degree rare in earlier poetry. On the other side are representations of landscapes without underlying order, as masses of beautiful and discontinuous detail. This leads to the question, posed and left undecided in a famous essay by Liu Zongyuan, regarding the existence of a creator, a purposeful intelligence behind the phenomena of the natural world.

This second essay is restricted to representations of the

order of the physical world, but similar questions regarding
purposeful order also arise in events in the human world.
"Interpreting," the third essay, discusses the Mid-Tang tendency to offer hypothetical explanations for phenomena that
either run contrary to received wisdom or try to account for
situations usually thought not to require explanation. Unsup-
ported by proof or textual authority, such singular interpretations were often tinged with either irony or madness. In this
way interpretation came to be understood as a subjective act,
determined less by the phenomenon interpreted than by the
motives and circumstances of the interpreter. Mid-Tang self-
awareness of this new, more subjectively motivated sense of
interpretation can be seen in two poetic attempts by Bai Juyi
to console himself after the death of his infant daughter: he
understands his endeavors to "be philosophical" about her
death as mere consolation, as truths that are used by a subject for other motives and are inadequate to contain the reality of feeling.

When carried out at the level of pure play, such subjective
acts of interpretation are wit. "Wit and the Private Life" treats
playfully inflated interpretations of domestic spaces and leisure activities as a discourse of private valuation, articulated
against commonsense values. Such values and meanings, offered in play, belong to the poet alone, and they create an effective private sphere distinct from the totalizing aspect of
Chinese moral and social philosophy, in which even solitary
and domestic behavior are part of a hierarchy of public values. To offer an example, when a fifth-century official left the
court to live as a recluse in the mountains, the ostensibly private decision could be, and often was understood as, a political statement; when the Mid-Tang poet wittily claimed complete devotion to his bamboo grove or his pet crane on his day
off, his playful excess broke free of public and political
meaning. It should not be surprising that this realm of play
usually concerns the poet's possessions. These texts weave
together ownership, subjective interpretation, and the exclu-

sion of others, whose commonsense perspective prevents them from seeing the value that the poet claims.

The poet who produces small dramas of contentment and amusement in his miniature garden, celebrating the moment in poetry, has already made an important change in the assumptions about how poetry was composed: rather than a poetry responding directly to experience, here experience is staged and the space physically arranged for the sake of composing poetry. "Ideas of Poetry and Writing in the Early Ninth Century" addresses some fundamental changes in the way writing, especially the writing of poetry, was represented in the Mid-Tang.

Already in the technical poetics of the eighth century we find acknowledgment of an interval between an occasioning experience and the writing of the poem. The relation of poetic composition to experience is described as a reenvisagement after the fact. By the early ninth century, the putatively organic link between extra-poetic experience and composition was no longer assumed. The basic material of poetry was the couplet, understood as a *trouvaille*; the couplet was worked on and framed within a poem by reflective craft. Such a view of poetic composition, however unsurprising in the context of the history of Western poetics, represented an important alternative within Chinese poetics, where the paramount value of authenticity had earlier been guaranteed by a proximity of poetic response, if not an absolute immediacy. By the early ninth century, the poem could be thought of as something constructed, rather than an involuntary expression, and what was represented in the poem was a scene of art rather than of the empirical world. This quintessentially "poetic" scene was often described as being "beyond"—beyond the words or the images that appeared to the ordinary senses. But in a famous description of the Mid-Tang poet Li He's process of composition, we also see the poem as an object to be shaped and possessed, no less an imaginative yet tangible construction than the little garden: each day the poet rides out, gets couplets and lines by inspiration, writes them down and throws them into a bag; each evening he takes the passages out and works them into poems.

The two final essays treat classical tales from the new culture of romance that took shape late in the eighth century. The essay entitled "Romance" takes up "Huo Xiaoyu's Story," a tale of love and betrayal, and discusses the phenomenon in the context of issues raised in "Wit and the Private Life," as an example of private valuation that tries to create a space for experience protected from the larger society and its demands. In contrast to the witty poet celebrating his garden, the commitment of the love affair is not pure play; its private domain inevitably comes into conflict with society and is disrupted. Here, however, we see clearly the presence of an audience that watches, judges, and ultimately intervenes in the ostensibly private love story. In the end, the culture of romance does not belong to lovers but to a community that reads such stories and is represented within them. In stories of romance we see that such a community, though composed of people who apparently belong to the world of public social values, supports the private values of romance.

"Conflicting Interpretations: 'Yingying's Story'" takes up the most famous of all Tang tales. Yingying, the heroine, and her lover Zhang are maternal cousins who might have legitimately married, but they are drawn into the Mid-Tang culture of passionate and unsanctioned romance, which ends, as romances often do, with Zhang deserting Yingying. Each of the lovers is an interpreter, trying to guide the narrative according to his or her own plot, and each makes a claim on the audience to judge in his or her favor. But the lovers' interpretations of events cancel each other out, and we are left with a situation unique in Tang narrative, in which judgment is called for, yet remains uncertain. Again the love story is situated within the context of a larger community that gossips, produces poems on the affair, and deliberates on how Zhang's behavior is to be judged.

The Mid-Tang was both a unique moment in Chinese literary culture and a beginning. Many phenomena that can be followed through the Song and the succeeding dynasties make their first appearance in the Mid-Tang. In many ways Mid-Tang writers seem intellectually closer to the great Song intellectuals two centuries later than to High Tang writers just a few decades earlier. The pride in singular interpretation, as opposed to the restatement of received knowledge, remained a constant in intellectual culture thereafter.[2] The fascination with miniatures and small domestic spaces for witty interpretation became the basis of a complex private culture of leisure activities that took its characteristic form in the Song.[3] Not only did the culture of romance continue, Tang tales of romance were continually retold and elaborated, as later writers tried to come to terms with the problems they posed. And when the great Song writer Su Shi saw a painting of a beautiful landscape, his response was not simply a desire to visit the spot and experience it directly; in "Written on a Painting of Layered Cliffs and a Misty River in the Collection of Wang Dingguo" 書王定國所藏煙江疊嶂圖, aesthetic idyll becomes a speculative purchase.

> 不知人間何處有此境，徑欲往買二頃田。
>
> I know not where in the mortal world such a
>   realm exists,
> but I want to go there right off and buy two
>   acres of fields.

In ways large and small, writers begin to assert their particular claim over a range of objects and activities: my land, my style, my interpretation, my garden, my particular beloved.

[2] Rote repetition of authoritative interpretation remained part of the tradition, but it was not as highly valued as producing a new interpretation.

[3] When I say "private culture," I do not mean that it belonged to the individual alone; if not shared with a group of like-minded friends, it was published to appeal to the like-minded. Nevertheless, this sphere of activity was understood as radically distinct not only from the claims of the state but also from the pragmatic claims of family.

Periods like the Mid-Tang are supposed to have dates. These essays concentrate on writing roughly between the years 791 and 825, though earlier and later works are also included. We know that periods are actually blurred centers that have no clear edges, but our geographical impulse to draw boundaries, to prevent unpossessed space, is instinctively transferred to our maps of history. To tell a good historical story we at least need a beginning.

Any account of the Mid-Tang leads back to Han Yu, the master storyteller whose accounts of literary and cultural history shaped all subsequent accounts.[4] Han Yu's most famous cultural narrative focuses on Han Yu himself, at the forefront of a Confucian revival. His morally engaged prose, *guwen* 古文 or "old-style prose," was meant to be an adequate vehicle for the restoration of Confucian values. To place Han Yu's account in a narrative of beginnings, let us date the Mid-Tang from 791–92, when Han Yu, Meng Jiao, Li Guan, and a number of other intellectuals came together in Chang'an to take the *jinshi* examination. Han Yu and Li Guan passed in 792. Two other important Mid-Tang writers, Liu Zongyuan and Liu Yuxi, passed the following year.

If we take this as the "beginning" of the Mid-Tang, it is not out of an excessive respect for Han Yu's authority, but because his brilliant staging of an important cultural moment eventually became a powerful agent of change. I say "eventually" because, even though Han Yu had large ambitions, he had no idea he was beginning something called the "Mid-Tang" or what that would mean. Beginnings take on their full meaning only retrospectively; you first have to know what it was that was begun. Nevertheless, despite large disparities in

---

[4] The literary term "Mid-Tang," dating from the early Ming, originally applied to the history of poetry and began with the aftermath of the An Lushan Rebellion (the late 750s) or the death of Du Fu (770); that is, the beginning of the "Mid-Tang" was a function of when the literary historian chose to end the "High Tang." Yet the image of High Tang poetry, focusing on Li Bai and Du Fu, was the creation of Han Yu and other Mid-Tang writers.

age—Meng Jiao was born in 751, and Li He in 790—the groupings of writers that formed in the next three and a half decades constituted a distinctive generation in a way that writers of the preceding three and a half decades had not.

The profound changes that appeared in Mid-Tang literature occurred at the same time as Han Yu's remarkable abrogation of continuous history: Han Yu declared himself and his moment a turning point in Chinese culture, a leap across more than a millennium to resume the Confucian tradition that had fallen into error and corruption after Mencius.[5] However important this claim may have been in the history of Confucianism, such a self-authorizing relation to the past formally embodied a new relation to many received traditions. Such a sense of being a generation of transformation and renewal sustained a variety of changes and new interests that were independent of the initial call for Confucian cultural regeneration.

The young men who came together in Chang'an in the early 790s articulated a rhetoric of urgency and crisis, an insistence that something needed to be done to restore literature and, through the restoration of literature, to restore cultural values. These men were generous in praising each other's work and were convinced that they held the solution to the ills of the land. The *fugu* 復古 ("restore antiquity") motifs and moral urgency of Han Yu, Meng Jiao, and Li Guan do not represent the entirety of the Mid-Tang; in fact, they are only a small part of the complex whole. Their significance seems rather to have been in the very act of instituting a generation, of declaring change and dividing history.

Many have tried to argue for the uniqueness of the political and social circumstances that gave these writers their sense of urgency. The problem with such an argument, posed as an adequate causal explanation, is that political and social

---

[5] The obvious European analogy is the Reformation, where the reformers claimed to cross over continuous Catholic tradition to pick up and continue the "true" Christianity of the early Church.

circumstances had been far worse in the Tang without producing a similar sense of urgency among writers. Neither the overthrow of the dynasty by Empress Wu, nor the rampant corruption of the decade following her death, nor the devastation of the country during the An Lushan Rebellion, nor the utter impotence of the government through most of the remaining century and a half of the Tang provoked such a feeling of crisis in writers (with a few exceptions, notably the poetry of Du Fu). We can properly say that Han Yu and his friends perceived an urgency in the present, but that tells us nothing about why they came together at that particular moment.

It would be wiser to offer historical context rather than causal explanations. There seems to have been a particular disillusionment in the early part of Dezong's reign (780–804). The reign began with great hopes for the restoration of the power of the central government out of the ruins of the post-rebellion period. These hopes quickly were shattered by Dezong's abject humiliation at the hands of the regional military commissioners (*jiedushi* 節度使) in 783. His ambitions chastened, Dezong became an unattractive imperial figure, and the ministries of the Daoist Li Mi and his successor, Dou Shen, did little to solve the empire's fiscal and political crises. The year 792 may well have seemed a new occasion for hope, as the great statesman Lu Zhi began what was to be a brief period as chief minister.

Traditional China had its political and economic pragmatists, but their writings were never popular with the historians who controlled the story of the past. Traditional intellectuals, especially in the Tang, tended to see political, social, and economic crises as symptoms of a cultural crisis, and cultural crisis was often conceived as a crisis of language and representation. Although far from unique to Dezong's reign, there was a debasement of imperial language during that period, for example, in the way it was so skillfully deployed by Lu Zhi to negotiate the survival of the dynasty in 783. Lu Zhi spent the coinage of imperial symbolism lavishly at a time when the royal house lacked the more reliable currencies of power: military force and hard cash. He used honors and what can only be called dynastic "futures," incomes and privileges that could be realized only by the stabilization of the dynasty. To those who believed in the ancient Confucian principle of "getting the names right," *zhengming* 正名, the period must have been a nightmare, with honorific titles and merits widely distributed to appease brute power and with regional bureaucratic appointments made hereditary under duress. The dead metaphor of debased currency should be kept in mind here: there was verbal inflation. The "words" by which roles in the Confucian state were realized had become hollow.

The Mid-Tang sea change took place against the backdrop of a perceived crisis of language and representation. The responses to this crisis were diverse yet linked by the recurrent concerns addressed in the following essays. Perhaps the most we can say of such moments in the history of a civilization is that "something happened." The magnitude of the event is always larger than the stories we can tell about it. But limited stories are our only way to come to terms with the greater phenomenon.

❖

Singularity and Possession

The assumption of an intense relation between verbal representations and the political or social order is one of the most striking characteristics of imperial Chinese civilization. The medieval elaborations of this assumption went far beyond the core Confucian principle of "getting the names right," *zheng-ming* 正名, a propriety of linguistic usage that ensured social and moral propriety. One formulation of that relation was a naive theory of reflection—that representations "reflected" the political and social order. Such a claim, which admits vast theoretical variation in the precise objects and modalities of reflection, is far from unique to China, and it remains with us today. The alternative formulation was not uniquely Chinese, but it had special historical weight in the Chinese tradition: this was the proposition that good representations can or should transform the political and social order. The most famous modern writer of fiction, Lu Xun, gave up medicine and became a writer in order to save China for just this reason.

The urgency apparent in the literary values of the "restoration of antiquity," *fugu* 復古, on the part of Han Yu 韓愈 (768–824) and his group depended on this assumption. In a different way the "New *Yuefu*," *Xin yuefu* 新樂府, of Bai Juyi 白居易 (772–846) and his friends followed from the same assumption. The clear representation of moral issues and their consequences for society would call forth and strengthen the innate moral sense of all readers, clarifying ethical issues and changing behavior.

In any system of representation positions tend to occur in sets, and the urgency with which a position is presented binds it to particular antitheses.[1] The assertion of the moral efficacy of representations in works of the Han Yu group and the Bai Juyi group is bound to a more significant particular countercase. Here, for what I believe is the first time on a large scale, we find the proposition that the "good" writer (with ambiguity between the morally "good" and "good" in a purely literary sense) will necessarily be ignored or actively rejected by society.

In more moderate versions, such as Bai Juyi's "Reading Zhang Ji's 'Old *Yuefu*,'" 讀張籍古樂府 (21744), the good writer is simply unappreciated and left to grow old in isolation.[2] In the most extreme formulations, as were offered repeatedly by Meng Jiao 孟郊 (751–814), "good" writing provokes the violent hostility of others and ultimately destroys the writer (19727).

> 本望文字達，今因文字窮。
>
> I had once hoped for triumph in writing,
> but now through writing I am in desperate
>   straits.

Qiong 窮, translated as "in desperate straits," combines impoverishment with a sense of being at the end of one's rope, having no recourse. Or in the still more extreme poem by Meng Jiao, "Tormented" 懊惱 (19755), a general term for reflective reading, "chewing over," *jujue* 咀嚼, becomes uncomfortably linked with literary cannibalism:

> 惡詩皆得官，好詩空抱山。
> 抱山空殗殗，終日悲顏顏。

---

[1] Note that I have specified *particular* antitheses. Any position, formulated with a sufficient level of abstraction, could be bound to a very large number of potential antitheses. Any actual position achieves direction and definition through the particular antitheses or countercases to which it is bound. Each countercase is, of course, itself also a position to which the first position serves as one possible countercase.

[2] All Tang poems are identified by their number in Hiraoka Takeo et al., *Tōdai no shihen* (Kyoto, 1964–65).

好詩更相嫉，劍戟生牙關。
前賢死已久，猶在咀嚼間。
以我殘杪身，清峭養高閑。
求閑未得閑，眾誚瞋虤虤。

Bad poets all win public office,
the good poet only clings to the hills.
Clings to the hills, shivering cold,
grieving in misery all the day through.
A good poet, what's more, wins their spite,
swords and pikes grow out of their teeth.
Good men of the past are long dead,
yet I still am chewing over them.
With this last tip of my life
pure and austere, I cultivated peace.
I sought peace but found no peace—
the packs mock me, glaring, snarling.

The politically and socially successful writer of two centuries later, Ouyang Xiu 歐陽修 (1007–72), asserted of good writing: "Skill follows from being driven to desperate straits," *qiong er hou gong* 窮爾後工. This argument is given explicitly to refute Ouyang Xiu's reformulation of Meng Jiao's position: "Poetry can drive a person to desperate straits," *shi neng qiong ren* 詩能窮人.

This is not so much a rupture of the assumption of a necessary relation between representation and society as its inversion or perversion. Rather than morally transforming society through writing, the good person is cast out, and the warped condition of the social body is reflected in his personal suffering. One of the most peculiar statements of this can be found in the third of Meng Jiao's "Laments for Yuan Lushan" 弔元魯山 on an eighth-century Confucian exemplar (20035):

君子不自蹇，魯山蹇有因。
苟含天地秀，皆是天地身。
天地蹇既甚，魯山道莫伸。
天地氣不足，魯山食更貧。
始知補元化，竟須得賢人。

The good man is not by nature lame;
that Lushan was lame had a cause.
Whoever embodies the flower of Earth and
    Heaven,
will have Earth and Heaven as his body.
Since Earth and Heaven were utterly lame,
the Way of Lushan could not stretch out.
The vital force of Earth and Heaven was inade-
    quate,
so Lushan ate ever more poorly.
Now I know that to patch the gap in Transfor-
    mation,
a worthy man had, at last, to be found.

This is reflection theory with a vengeance, and Meng Jiao saw his own experience and writing in much the same terms. In the fourth poem of the same series, difference, even the difference of moral superiority, results in rejection by society (20036).

一聲苟失所，衆憾來相排。

If but one voice lose its place,
the crowd is dissatisfied and drives him away.

When the "proper sound," *zhengsheng* 正聲, appears in a fallen world, it does not redeem the world by bringing it to harmony; rather, it becomes a jarring dissonance that must be silenced. In this same spirit Han Yu would write to Li Yi about his theory of prose composition: if anyone were pleased by what he wrote, he would know that it was still imperfect.

This points us to one of the most significant literary transformations of the Mid-Tang: a notion of identity, especially "authentic" (*zhen* 眞) identity, as singularity. Moreover, such singularity often appears as a negative movement, an exclusion of others or by others. I use the term "singularity," rather than the comfortable but loaded word "individuality," to stress the element of pain, isolation, and alienation in this moment of distinction. There may be pride and an aggressive claim of superiority, but often we hear the voices of the "others" laughing, mocking, disbelieving, and sometimes making the snarling sounds of beasts. Singularity is not only repeat-edly thematized in Mid-Tang writing, it also appears in the willfully singular styles of Mid-Tang writers. The singular style might provoke the surprise, contempt, and rejection of others, or it might win admiration. Singularity was not uni-versal individuation; it presumed the existence of conven-tional, normative, and often morally suspect "others." Moral and literary superiority would now be demonstrated not by perfection within socially approved norms but by its very al-ienation from those norms.[3]

The singularity of the person is closely related to a new interest in ownership and possession, which, like identity, is conceptualized in terms of the exclusion of others. Although singularity primarily concerns one person, the same form can be seen on the corporate level, with a singular group of excep-tional men that excludes the "common," or an ideological community that excludes the heterodox, or even a China that is, for the first time, conceived in terms of excluding the for-eign, as is proposed in Han Yu's famous "Memorial on the Buddha's Bone." Whether at the level of the individual or the community, the singular entity tries to demarcate a space that belongs to it; it possesses objects and engages in prac-tices that are "proper" to it. But to achieve this, there must be "others" on the outside, who would like to intrude into the space and corrupt its practices.

It is important here to acknowledge the numerous exem-plary figures from earlier in the Chinese tradition who repre-sent variations on identity as singularity and contributed in part to the Mid-Tang construction of singular identity. The ancient poet Qu Yuan 屈原, perhaps more than any other, in-sistently returned to the theme of his alienation from all other

---

[3] The most famous statement of this position is found in the "First Letter in Answer to Mr. Li" 答李生第一書 by Han Yu's younger disciple Huangfu Shi 皇甫湜, in which he argues of writing that distinction in the positive sense is necessarily "strange," *qi* 奇, and "bizarre," *guai* 怪. Both terms, particularly "bizarre," carried potentially negative associations that are here made positive.

human beings. Tao Qian 陶潛 (365–427) is somewhat similar in claiming to have been compelled by his nature to renounce his normative social role. We might include the eccentrics of the Wei and Jin. But among these figures, singularity itself was a central value only for Qu Yuan. What distinguishes the Mid-Tang is that we have a value shared by many intellectuals in a particular age.[4] In the Mid-Tang singularity is not a condition without content, as was the case with Qu Yuan, but an entire repertoire of singular traits.

Before the Mid-Tang a limited set of differentiated typologies was adequate to describe a writer's identity. The writer was a personality type working through a genre, with individual differentiation occurring in the particularity of experience. Although Li Bai 李白 (701–62) and, in a different way, Du Fu 杜甫 (712–70) began to move in the direction of identity through the assertion of singularity, there was generally no particular importance attached to being unique, essentially distinct from others.[5] Furthermore, we should keep in mind that the canonization of Li Bai and Du Fu was an essentially Mid-Tang phenomenon. In the Mid-Tang the distinction of singularity *was* important to many writers.[6]

As authenticity became increasingly linked to singular

---

[4] To claim a beginning in the Chinese tradition immediately invites the counterclaim of an earlier beginning. The eccentrics of the third and fourth centuries showed a similar negative relation to social norms, but they did not establish among themselves a system of individuated stylistic personalities. By the Mid-Tang the earlier "eccentric" was already a stylized type.

[5] Literary culture before the Mid-Tang did, of course, recognize distinction in a relative sense: a poet might be "exceptional" or "stand out from the crowd." But such distinction was not linked to a singular style, in turn linked to a singular nature, as was the case with a Meng Jiao or a Li He.

[6] Perhaps the most ruthless statement of differentiation from an earlier age awaited the middle of the ninth century when Li Shangyin, in his "Offhand Compositions," 漫成五首, looked back on the Early Tang masters and contemptuously commented that in his time one could see only "ableness in parallelism," *duishu neng* 對屬能. The once-positive *neng* 能, "skill," here has become the contemptuous "ableness."

identity during the Mid-Tang, in literary language a growing awareness of the cliché and a heightened attention to conformity carried strong associations of falseness. In both the Han Yu and the Bai Juyi group there was an intense suspicion of "hollow verbiage," *kongwen* 空文. Earlier *fugu* advocates had opposed ornamentation in writing, associating it with frivolity and moral corruption. The Mid-Tang intellectuals echoed this, but added a new distrust of conventional but false words, words that did not match the facts. Again and again Meng Jiao prefaced commonplace notions with "who claims?" *shei wei* 誰謂, or "in vain is it said," *tuyan* 徒言. Meng Jiao would take an authoritative commonplace, such as the claim that human beings are the most "numinous," *ling* 靈, of creatures, and refute it (20031):

> 徒言人最靈，白骨亂縱橫。

> In vain is it said that man is most numinous—
> his white bones lie scattered in disarray.

The text Meng Jiao was refuting here is the *Classic of Documents*, the *Shujing*. It was not that poets had never noticed and lamented unburied bones before, but earlier writers tended to use authoritative texts to *confirm* their experience, and not to call to mind authoritative texts that contradicted experience.[7]

The general distrust of conventional writing, which was to become such a conspicuous feature of late imperial culture, first appeared prominently in this period. To praise the unrecorded virtues of a simple county magistrate, Bai Juyi began with a telling countercase in "Setting up Stelae" 立碑 (21822).

> 勳德既下衰，文章亦陵夷。
> 但見山中石，立作路旁碑。
> 銘勳悉太公，敘德皆仲尼。
> 復以多爲貴，千言直萬貲。
> 爲文彼何人，想見下筆時。

---

[7] In many ways such challenges to the Confucian Classics are a measure of the new kind of authority being granted to the Classics.

但欲愚者悅，不思賢者嗤。
豈獨賢者嗤，仍傳後代疑。
古石蒼苔字，安知是愧詞。

Since virtue and merit have gone into decay,
writings as well are in decline.
One sees only the rocks of the mountains
set up as stelae by the road.
The merits inscribed are all like Taigong's;
accounts of virtues are always like Confucius.
What's more, it is valued by the amount,
a thousand words worth a fortune of ten
    thousand.
Who was the person who wrote that text?
I imagine him setting his brush to work.
He wanted only that fools be pleased
and gave no thought to good men's scorn.
The problem is not just good men's scorn—
passed on, later ages will not be sure.
Words with green moss on ancient stone—
how will they know these are shameless words?

"Setting up Stelae" goes on to praise a certain Magistrate Ju of Wangjiang County, whose virtues are naturally remembered by the common folk he governed so well. But the message of the poem is ultimately more pessimistic, imagining stelae filled with polite lies, mossy with age, and deceiving readers of the future. We see here clearly the first glimmerings of Song and late imperial distrust of textual authority and the written tradition.[8]

The alternative to a false and debased writing would be the text that somehow embodied truth and moral authority. Polite comparisons to Taigong, the chief advisor to King Wen of the Zhou, and to Confucius were clearly no longer adequate. Li Shangyin's 李商隱 (813?–58) famous "Han Yu's Stele" 韓碑 (29148) tropes on the ratios of text, memory, and truth that were a concern in Bai Juyi's "Setting up Stelae."

[8] See Supplementary Texts for Zhao Yi's (1727–1814) third "Poems on My Dwelling in the Rear Park," in which the Qing poet cheerfully describes writing an inscription of the sort Bai Juyi describes.

Here Han Yu's famous inscription praising Pei Du's achievements in the Huaixi campaign is effaced by imperial command, and a new, false inscription is written over it. But the true inscription, Li Shangyin tells us in the following passage, has already entered the hearts of people and is preserved there.

> 句奇語重喻者少，讒之天子言其私。
> 長繩百尺拽碑倒，粗砂大石相磨治。
> 公之斯文若元氣，先時已入人肝脾。
> 湯盤孔鼎有述作，今無其器存其詞。

> The lines were strange, the diction grave,
>   those who grasped the meaning, few;
> they maligned it to the Emperor
>   and said it represented private motives.
> With a long rope of a hundred feet
>   they pulled the stele over,
> and on the great stone with coarse gravel
>   they ground the inscription away.
> But the Master's Cultural Writing
>   is like the primal force
> and before that time had already
>   entered people's hearts.
> Tang's basin, Confucius' tripod
>   had texts written thereon,
> but though these vessels now are gone,
>   the words on them survive.

It particularly significant that in writing "Han Yu's Stele" Li Shangyin adopted a versified version of Han Yu's own style, as every contemporary and subsequent reader would have recognized. Herein was the great paradox of the singular style: the style that carries authority because it is not conventional and is marked with the identity and authentic convictions of the writer can be appropriated by others. When appropriated, it will be forever marked as "Han Yu's style." This style "belongs to" Han Yu, and a fully developed sense of possession makes possible borrowing, inheritance, and attempted theft.

Conformity to shared social norms, whether in behavior

or writing, may give rise to an impression of falseness and in-authenticity, but by its very nature such conformity avoids troubling issues that arise from singularity. Conformity to particular social norms is not said to arise from inner compulsion, nor can one claim to have made the social norm oneself. Social norms are received from others, and even when they become second nature and are reproduced spontaneously, they are externally confirmed. A discourse of singularity, in contrast, poses an unanswerable question: Is the manifestation of singularity involuntary or voluntary, natural or artificial? It can be shown that this is a theoretically meaningless question which can never be answered; it *was*, however, a real question for writers and intellectuals in the Mid-Tang. Either the poet is helplessly expressing his singular identity, or he is self-conscious and in complete control. We often find these two contradictory "answers" conjoined. In either case the product belongs uniquely to the poet and bears his signature in ways that are impossible with purely normative forms of literary expression.

Bai Juyi often insisted on the spontaneity of his nature and his poetry, that it was produced by inner compulsion. In the following poem the signature of spontaneity is clumsiness, a failure to conform to literary norms that leads to rejection of his verse by others. The outcast poet then constructs a small, imaginative community of other exceptional writers, displaced from him in time or space.

What Came to Mind When Chanting
My Poems 自吟拙什因有所懷 (21995)

懶病每多暇，暇來何所爲。
未能抛筆硯，時作一篇詩。
詩成淡無味，多被衆人嗤。
上怪落聲韻，下嫌拙言詞。
時時自吟詠，吟罷有所思。
蘇州及彭澤，與我不同時。
此外復誰愛，唯有元微之。
謫向江陵府，三年作判司。
相去二千里，詩成遠不知。

> Lazy and sickly, with much free time;
> when free time comes, what do I do?
> I can't put away my inkstone or brush,
> and sometimes write a poem or two.
> Poems finished are bland, lacking tang,
> and often much mocked by the public.
> They first complain that my rhymes
>   are off,
> they then deplore maladroit phrasing.
> I sometimes read them out to myself;
> when I finish, I feel a longing:
> The poets Tao Qian and Wei Yingwu
> were born in ages other than mine;
> Except for them whom do I love?—
> there is only Yuan Weizhi;
> He has gone off to Jiangling in exile,
> for three years to serve as subaltern.
> Two thousand leagues apart we are—
> so far he knows not when a poem is done.

If Bai Juyi here claims a casual, unreflective compulsion in composition, elsewhere he foregrounds the act of wit. Even in this poem we see his self-consciousness, writing "about" his indifference to literary norms rather than simply out of such indifference. Bai Juyi often portrays himself acting spontaneously, while at the same time laughing at himself for doing so, thus letting us know that he knows better. Spontaneity, manifested in clumsiness, has clearly become a value, but no less a value is the image of knowing urbanity.

Li He 李賀 (791–817) often presents a figure with a different quality of compulsion, a haunted compulsion, and he had a special affinity for characters driven by it.

A Long Song Follows a Short Song
長歌續短歌 (20745)

長歌破衣襟，短歌斷白髮。
秦王不可見，旦夕成內熱。
渴飲壺中酒，饑拔隴頭粟。
淒涼四月闌，千里一時綠。
夜峰何離離，明月落石底。

徘徊沿石尋，照出高峰外。
不得與之遊，歌成鬢先改。

Long songs ruined my clothing,
short songs snapped my white hair.
I cannot meet the King of Qin,
from dawn to dusk I have fever within.
Thirsty, I drink the wine in the jug;
hungry, I pull up the grain on the slope.
Dreary and chill the fourth month ends,
a thousand leagues in one instant green.
How clearly the peaks are ranged by night,
the bright moon falls to the foot of the stone.
I linger and chase it along the stone,
but it shines out beyond the highest peak.
I cannot go roaming together with it,
and my locks turn white ere my song is done.

Whether Li He's fever here is political, poetic, or fanned by his
dread of mortality, he represents himself as helplessly driven
by inexplicable forces within. But Li He was also a master
craftsman, recognized as such, and his style often bears the
signature of careful and reflective craft.[9] The distinction between singularity as inner compulsion, hence "genuine," and
singularity as mannerism, hence "artificial," is impossible to
draw.

    Cultural and literary historical periods are best under-
stood as matrices. These matrices are not aggregates of isolated qualities but sets composed of antithetical or contradictory terms and positions. Subsets of alternatives within the
matrix are the "issues," and it often seems that every compelling attempt to address an issue in some way includes both

---

[9] I use the term "signature of reflective craft" to refer to the way in
which certain kinds of styles were associated with conscious effort. Bai
Juyi may well have worked on the lines of his "spontaneous" poems
longer and with greater care than Li He, but such lines appear to the
reader as if they were truly spontaneous. Many of Li He's lines, on the
other hand, appear artful. As our later discussion will show, the *trouvaille* became a way of reconciling the unselfconscious and the artful,
instantaneity and duration.

alternatives. But issues do not stand alone: they are linked to other issues, sometimes aligned in parallel and sometimes collapsing to a single term in a new antithesis. Thus the opposed alternatives "compulsion" and "artistic control" collapse into versions of singular distinction when set in opposition to conventional norms.

Such opposed alternatives, the fact that certain questions are in play, mark the vitality of a period. Eventually the opposed alternatives are either forgotten or resolved, often into a new commonplace or image. This may be one way to define the close of an era. In the end, the Mid-Tang interest in the opposition between compulsion and artistic control merged in the notion of craft *as* artistic compulsion. This conjunction of compulsion and artifice comes together nicely in the fate of the word *kuyin* 苦吟. Originally, it meant "chanting poems out of pain," but by the second decade of the ninth century it had already taken on the meaning "painstaking composition." Somehow the extraliterary feeling of pain that led to composition was transferred to the intense labor of the act of composition itself.

The issue of singularity is closely aligned with the Mid-Tang discourse of possession and ownership. The rareness of questions of ownership in earlier literature suggests that their appearance in the Mid-Tang touches on concerns central to the period. The very idea of possession, that something "belongs to" someone, is crucial to this new notion of singular identity, what is "one's own" because it excludes others and, most of all, because it excludes the conventional, what is held in common.

One of the rare references to ownership of territory in earlier literature can be found in Wang Wei's 王維 (701–61) "Hollow by Meng's Walls" 孟城坳 the first poem of the "Wang Stream Collection" 輞川集.

> 新家孟城口，古木餘衰柳。
> 來者復爲誰，空悲昔人有。

> New home in a breach in Meng's walls,
> where of ancient trees remain dying willows.

Who will be those who are yet to come?—
pointless grief that men had it before.

Here Wang Wei writes of his own estate, and the inde-
terminacy of the referent in the final line—we do not know if
Wang himself is thinking of the previous owner or imagining
future visitors who will think of him—calls into question the
meaning of possession. The term used here is *you* 有: it is
"having" rather than specifically owning (for example, one
may "have a cup," *you bei* 有杯, without being the cup's legal
owner).

We might compare Wang Wei's poem to an apparently in-
nocuous quatrain by Han Yu, also treating the impermanence
of possession, on another estate. This is "Visiting the Mountain Estate of the Princess Taiping" 游太平公主山莊 (18080).
Princess Taiping, the daughter of Gaozong and the Empress
Wu, became one of the most powerful political figures in the
second reign of Zhongzong (705–10). Remembering her vast
estates in the region south of Chang'an recalled the extravagance of the early eighth century.

> 公主當年欲占春，故將臺榭壓成闌。
> 欲知前面花多少，直到南山不屬人。

> Back in those years the Princess
>   wanted spring as her own:
> on purpose she put terraces and kiosks
>   right up to the city's gates.
> If you would know how many flowers
>   she looked at before her—
> all the way to Mount Zhongnan
>   belonged to no one else.

The central terms here are *zhan* 占, "to occupy" or "hold
as one's own" and *shu* 屬, "to own" or "belong to." The oxymoronic "to have spring as all one's own," *zhanchun* 占春, is related to a commonplace in Mid-Tang poetry, variously formulated, with the master usually being some creature or plant
whose present figurative ownership recalled the absence of
past human owners. Here such impossible possession (who

can "own spring") is circumscribed as a past event, "back in those years," *dangnian* 當年. The desire, *yu* 欲, produces the assertion that her activities were "on purpose," *gu* 故. The princess covers territory with buildings in order to own nature or a season. The buildings are not merely the visible signs of her possession, they are also vistas from which she can observe spring. "Right up to," *ya* 壓, a poetic term for close proximity, is well chosen: her territory literally "presses hard upon" the city gates, allowing no intervening space through which others can freely pass and interrupt her vista.

In the second couplet Han Yu poses a hypothetical question and formulates it so as to allow him to give the answer that he wants. The question is not simply "how many flowers" she owned, but *qian mian* 前面, how many she saw before her. It is not pure possession but the contemplation of the magnitude of her possessions that she wishes. It is not merely ownership but a display of ownership for her enjoyment.

If one boundary of her territory lies against the walls of Chang'an, the final line sets the other limit of her dominion, Mount Zhongnan, visible in the distance south of Chang'an. The answer to the hypothetical question does not count the flowers: it is space defined by the exclusion of others, a space that "monopolizes" or "has as one's own," *zhan*, the spring scene. Hers is not a vista of flowers but a vista of possession.

Part of the pleasure of the poem is the way in which the poet contests that territory, visiting the princess's estate and intruding on her vanished dominion. It is easy to read this poem as a satire on early eighth-century excess, but like virtually all poems in the praise and blame tradition, it revels in precisely what it condemns. In place of the princess's legal dominion, the poet experiences an imaginative poetic dominion, standing for a while in her place and delighting in imagined possession through her imagined eyes. Ownership in the Mid-Tang often involves actual purchase, but physical possession becomes inextricable from ownership as the discursive act of staking a claim through words and an act of imagination.

It is impossible to know with certainty which poem is earlier, but Han Yu's poem on Princess Taiping's estate is obviously related to Bai Juyi's "Visiting Yunju Temple: To Mu Thirty-six, Local Landowner" 游雲居寺贈穆三十六地主 (22382) (dated 807).

亂峰深處雲居路，共踏花行獨惜春。
勝地本來無定主，大都山屬愛山人。

> In the deepest spots of tangled peaks
>   the road to Yunju Temple,
> we both go treading the flowers,
>   I alone feel bad about spring.
> Ever the most splendid sites
>   lack a permanent owner:
> by and large the mountain belongs
>   to the person who loves the mountain.

The use of the term "landowner," *dizhu* 地主, in the title is unusual. To refer to someone as *dizhu*, or to address a poem to someone who is a *dizhu*, is an acknowledgment of a fact usually suppressed in Tang literary representations: there was a structure of power and ownership in China distinct from a world composed of officials and peasants. A *dizhu* possesses land without working it, yet he is not attached to the state.[10] In this poem, whose playfulness scarcely conceals its rudeness, Bai Juyi poetically takes Mr. Mu's land away from him.

The heart of the second line is a moment of distinction: both men walk through the fallen flowers, but only one—obviously Bai Juyi himself—feels sad about spring's passage. "Feel bad about," *xi* 惜, is an interesting word: it suggests not simply feeling sad about loss but begrudging it, not wanting it to happen. A distinction is being drawn between legal terri-

---

[10] Although this question is usually excluded from literary representation, the question of landownership was a serious fiscal issue in the early ninth century, owing to the change in tax assessments from a head tax to a tax on the productivity of land in the late eighth century. Rich landowners found ways to keep their assessments low.

tory and territory to be experienced, "splendid sites," *shengdi* 勝地, available to sensibility. The local landowner wants the territory; the poet wants the territory as a site for experience. Thus Bai reminds the landowner of the impermanence of possession, and, with the equivocal vernacular "by and large," *dadou* 大都, allowing some small scope to the landowner's claim, Bai takes possession of the landscape for himself as "the person who loves the mountain," *aishan ren* 愛山人.

The argument is a neat one: by invoking the temporal limitations of possession, a place can be possessed only in the experience of caring about it—or, perhaps, in the more permanent representation of such an experience in a text.

The secret twist of the Bai Juyi poem is, however, "the person who loves the mountain," *aishan ren*, which inevitably recalls the "finding delight in the mountains," *leshan* 樂山, of the *Analects* (VI.21), the characteristic of a person "possessing fellow-feeling," *ren* 仁. By "feeling bad about spring," *xi chun* 惜春, Bai shows himself to have sensibility, the quality of "fellow-feeling," displaced into the physical world. Invoking Confucian kinship with the world, Bai asserts the Confucian moral order against the legal order of the landowner. But Bai says *aishan* and not *leshan*: it is not the simple "delight" in the mountains, but "love" or "doting fondness for"—someone who "delights in the mountains" does not necessarily want to hold on to the mountains, but someone who "loves the mountains" does. The Mid-Tang writer is beginning to hold on to things. As the poem explicitly says, Bai Juyi is staking a claim on the territory.

Like Han Yu, Bai Juyi confronts an owner and takes imaginative, poetic possession of a space. Though both claims are temporally restricted, such poetic assertions of title to space begin to become far less innocent than they seem at first glance. In the Mid-Tang we begin to encounter the notion that a poet can "occupy" a place by writing about it in a memorable way. If the poet embodies the place in words, others will not write about it; they will recognize that the representation of the place has become the poet's own. Inspired by someone else's poems on Jinling, a former capital of the Southern Dynasties, Liu Yuxi 劉禹錫 (772–842) wrote his famous set of poems, "Five Topics on Jinling" 金陵五題 (19273–77), describing the city even before visiting it personally. In the preface Liu proudly comments on Bai Juyi's response:

> When I was younger, I traveled in the southeast, but felt a lingering regret that I had never visited Moling [Jinling]. Later I became Governor of Liyang and would gaze toward it from afar. I chanced once to have a visitor who showed me "Five Topics on Jinling" he had written. With a faint smile I fell into thought, and these poems came to me in a flash. Later my friend Bai Juyi chanted them with an intense seriousness, swaying his head and sighing in appreciation a long time. He said, "After that line in 'The Rock' which goes, 'Tides dash on those empty walls, then turn back in stillness,' I am certain no later poet will try to write about the topic again." Although the other four are not as good as that one, they too do not fail to live up to what Bai said.

If empirical ownership is transitory, the poetic occupation of a place raises the possibility of permanent ownership: "no later poet will try to write about the topic again," *hou zhi shiren bu fu cuoci yi* 後之詩人不復措辭矣. A poem can inscribe experiential possession of the sort Bai Juyi claimed in his quatrain, and the momentary can become permanent (even if the experiential possession is purely imaginative, as Liu Yuxi's was). All later visitors will see it marked with old poems and experience the place through old poems. Permanent ownership of place can only be achieved textually.

One of the most interesting texts of purchase, "poetic" experience, and representation is Liu Zongyuan's 柳宗元 (773-819) "An Account of the Small Hill West of Gumu Pond" 鈷鉧潭西小丘記, which leads us to raise the question: Why does a person buy land? The most obvious answer is: in order to use it. One should, however, add a qualification: ownership must involve the power to transfer title or to pass on the land to one's descendants, to perpetuate one's ownership. If the state allots one land to use only for one's lifetime, one cannot say one "owns" it. This is important to our discussion because it is the counterpart of the transmission of representations, whether a memorable poem or a singular style. Far more than territory, these can be passed on to the future still bearing the "title" of the original owner.

In the Mid-Tang writers begin to buy land for experience. The aristocracy and great officials had done this earlier, often inviting poets to celebrate and thus perpetuate the display of their possessions. Liu Zongyuan buys land while in exile. It is not land he can use to produce wealth. Since it is in a remote place in Yongzhou, it seems unlikely that he intends to pass it on to his descendants. Most significant, he could surely have had the use of the land for experience without purchasing it; it seems likely that the previous owners would not have objected if he had visited the place as much as he pleased; and indeed, if Liu wrote about it, they would probably be able to get more money for it. Why, then, did Liu Zongyuan buy it? The only explanation is that he bought it in order to "own" it. Ownership has come to take on a value all its own. In Liu Zongyuan's peculiar phrasing: "I was attached to it, so I bought it," *yu lian er shou zhi* 余憐而售之. Such attachment to the place is very close to Bai Juyi's "loving the mountains," *aishan*.

Liu Zongyuan, *An Account of the Small Hill West of
Gumu Pond* (third of the "Eight Accounts of Yongzhou")

Eight days after I reached West Mountain, I was exploring about two hundred paces along the road that leads northwest from the mouth of the valley, and I found Gumu Pond. Twenty-five paces west of the pond, where the water flowed swift and deep, a fish-weir had been made. Above the fish-weir was a hill growing with trees and bamboo. Almost beyond counting were its rocks, which jutted out menacingly, rearing themselves aloft, spurning the earth in their emergence and rivaling one another in rare shapes. The ones that descended, interlocking downward from sharp clefts, seemed like cattle and horses watering at the creek. The ones that rose, thrusting rows of horns upward, seemed like bears climbing on a mountain.

The hill was so small it did not cover even an acre; one might have kept it packed in a basket. I asked the person in charge, who said, "This is land of the Tang family for which they have no use. They put it on the market, but couldn't sell it." I asked how much they wanted for it, and he said, "Only four hundred pieces of silver." I was attached to it, so I bought it. At the time Li Shenyuan and Yuan Keji had come along with me, and they were both overjoyed at such an unexpected turn of events. We each in turn went to get tools, scything away the undesirable plants and cutting down the bad trees, which we set fire to and burned. Then the fine trees stood out, the lovely bamboo were exposed, and the unusual rocks were revealed. When we gazed out from upon it, the heights of the mountains, the drifting of clouds, the currents of streams, and the cavorting of birds and beasts all cheerfully demonstrated their art and skill in performance for us below the hill. When we spread out our mats and lay down there, the clear and sharply defined shapes were in rapport with our eyes; the sounds of babbling waters were in rapport with our ears; all those things that went on forever in emptiness were in rapport with our spirits; and what was as deep and still as an abyss was in rapport with our hearts. In less than ten full days I had obtained two rare places. Even those who loved scenic spots in olden times may well never have been able to equal this.

I must say that if I were to transport this splendid scenery to Feng, Hao, Hu, or Duling, the nobility who are fond of excursions would rival one another to purchase it. Every day its price would increase by another thousand pieces of silver, and it would grow ever harder to afford. But now it is left forsaken in this province; as they pass by, farmers and fishermen think it worth nothing, and even with a price of only four hundred pieces it was left unpurchased for years on end. Yet I, together with Li Shenyuan and Yuan Keji, have been singularly delighted to get it. Isn't this a case of having a lucky encounter at last?! I wrote this on stone to celebrate this hill's lucky encounter.

Note that, though attracted by the natural beauty of the spot, Liu's first act on purchasing the hill is to clear it. He is buying the hill for the sake of the literary experience of the hill, an experience to be published and passed on. He was initially attracted to the wild hill, but the literary experience requires staging, clearing parts to mark it as his own, unifying the artifactual and the natural. Liu Zongyuan is reveling in the *fact* of possession, and his license to modify the space and mark it as his own.

Unlike the Princess Taiping, Liu Zongyuan does not build structures on the land. He has located and circumscribed a space in the middle of a wilderness; by this process of location and delimitation of space, the oxymoronic "purchase of Nature" becomes possible. Liu's first impression of Gumu Hill was in terms of its resemblance to wild animals. Note what happens, however, once the hill becomes a possession: "When we gazed out from upon it, the heights of the mountains, the drifting of clouds, the currents of streams, and the cavorting of birds and beasts all cheerfully demonstrated their art and skill in performance for us below the hill." Nature is imaginatively transformed into a work of performance art for the owners; purchased space seems to make spontaneous shapes and motions into a form of display that is normally hired. There is a reciprocal relation between empirical ownership, which brings the right to manipulate and modify the physical world, and acts of imaginative interpretation.

This joy in ownership is most clearly seen in the speculative transportation of the hill to the capital, where, in the proximity of others who could appreciate such places, its price would rise. Part of the experience of possession is displaying it to others and having others want the thing possessed. This is represented in the account as Liu's making a profit on the transaction—if only an imaginative profit. Here "the person who loves the mountain," *aishan ren*, the person with the sensibility to appreciate a place, gets an empirical bargain. Possession, in order to give the full satisfaction of the experience of possession, must be displayed and passed on. Thus Liu Zongyuan completes his possession of the hill discursively, through a text. The legal deed is arranged with the Tangs; the written "account" is his cultural deed of ownership.

The idea of ownership, by which I mean ownership as a pleasure that transcends merely having for one's use, is a great mystery. A thing or place is stamped with a particular person's name. In the wonderful English phrase, one "has title" to it. And it is not extravagant to see how closely this is related to the singularly individual style. The pleasure of having a style or owning something is the capacity to display possession to others and to exclude them. Both are deeply tied to questions of mortality and are tested in having the power to pass them on to others. Possession of objects or land is inferior here, because the processes of transmission are historically unstable, and legitimacy of ownership can be proved only by a text, which traces the sequence of possession back to an original owner. To possess a singular style or a text that memorably represents an experience or a place is a more secure means of transmitting ownership to the future. If the Mid-Tang canonized Li Bai and Du Fu among High Tang poets, the reason may have been that their singular poetic styles, more than those of any of their High Tang contemporaries, could be recognized as belonging to them alone.

In the Mid-Tang, and in its reading of what would become the High Tang, we find a new and familiar sense of identity, which is closely tied to empirical and discursive acquisition and possession. "Ownership" may be understood as a cultural and discursive phenomenon as much as an economic phenomenon; that is, it involves the celebration and display of possession, which itself becomes "cultural capital." It is the production of value. Liu Zongyuan spent family money to buy land that, in Tang terms, was in the middle of nowhere, in the wilderness of his exile. He discursively "improves" that land, gives it value where it had none. The land of Gumu Hill will not feed Liu Zongyuan or his descendants, but the text, which is a text about acquisition, is potentially a more reliable piece of cultural capital and may contribute to the aggrandizement of both the author and his descendants.

❖

Reading the Landscape

In the summer or early autumn of 806, Han Yu made an excursion into the mountains near Chang'an and wrote his famous long poem "South Mountains" 南山詩 (17790) in praise of the landscape there. At the conclusion of an extended passage describing the variety of the mountains' shapes, Han Yu made an explicit comparison to the hexagrams of the *Classic of Changes*:

> 或如龜坼兆，或若卦分繇。
> 或前橫若剝，或後斷若姤。
>
> Some, like the omens cracked in tortoise-shell,
> some, like the hexagrams, divided into lines.
> Some are like Bo, stretching across up front,
> some are like Gou, broken in the back.[1]

The season must have been ripe for discovering textual inscription in landscape; that same autumn, experimenting with a new kind of linked verse, *lianju* 聯句, together with his friend Meng Jiao, Han Yu capped Meng's line (43194):

> 窯煙冪疏島
>
> Smoke from kilns veils distant isles

with a striking and beautiful image:

---

[1] Read from the bottom, the hexagram Bo consists of five broken lines, with an unbroken line on top. Gou has one broken line on the bottom, with the lines above unbroken.

沙篆印迴平

Sandy seal-script imprinted on turning flats

This imprint was probably the track of a person or an animal because the younger poet Li He, returning to his home at Changgu in 811, recalled this same image and specified the source of the imprint (20809):[2]

汰沙好平白，立馬印青字。

Washed sands nicely white and flat,
the standing horse imprints green characters.

Some decades later, writing on his family estate at Vermilion Bank, *Zhupo* 朱坡, Du Mu 杜牧 (803–52) picked up the same "impression," probably from Li He's poem (28105):

沙渚印麛蹄

Sandy isles imprinted by hooves of fawns

Du Mu, the Late Tang poet, has made one significant change in the image: while keeping the figurative verb "imprint," *yin* 印, he has dropped the explicit comparison of the impression to the written word.

The image of oracular cracks and hexagrams appearing in the landscape on "South Mountains" differs, however, in significant ways from the image of characters imprinted on the landscape in Han Yu and Meng Jiao's "South of the City

---

[2] Although he could not have known of Han Yu's line, at roughly the same time Liu Zongyuan in his Yongzhou exile wrote a long descriptive landscape poem answering Liu Yuxi's "An Account of My Feelings at Wuling." This poem contains the line (18423): "Moisture prints the gravel by Brocade Creek," *ru yin Jinxi sha* 濡印錦溪砂. Liu Zongyuan uses *sha* 砂 with a stone radical, but it is essentially the same word as *sha* 沙, "sand," as in the other passages. In the second of his "Autumn Cares" 秋懷 (19738), Meng Jiao takes the image indoors, with his bedridden body as the seal making the imprint: "On my mat is printed the text of sickness," *xishang yin bingwen* 席上印病文. The Chinese verb *yin* 印, "imprint," is more strongly figurative in the original than in English, where "print" (e.g., footprint) is a dead metaphor. *Yin* primarily suggests the action of a seal.

Linked Verse" 城南聯句 and Li He's "Changgu" 昌谷詩, quoted
above. These differences point to a deeper division in the representation of Nature in the poems. The figure of the hexagram is one of a natural pattern emerging to the surface from
within. The particular hexagram makes sense only as part of
a complete system that is already known; the detail refers us
to the totality that contains it and gives it meaning. In contrast, the images of characters imprinted on the sand are
transitory and fragmentary impressions that come to the
landscape from the outside. They are discontinuous signs of
passage, themselves noted in passage, patterns as words that
cannot be read.

Extended representations of landscape embody assumptions about the natural order (or the absence thereof). The
natural order that had been part and parcel of medieval poetic rhetoric had provided earlier poets an unreflective sense
of security regarding Nature's intelligibility. Parallelism and
other conventions of poetic language were the literary mani-
festations of a binary cosmology and natural science: a couplet on mountains followed a couplet on waters, a line on
hearing matched a line on seeing, the upward gaze balanced
a downward gaze. Both Nature and rhetoric were productive
and reliable mechanisms.[3] Although this medieval rhetoric
continued to be practiced in the Mid-Tang, for some writers
the order of the landscape and indeed of all Nature became a
question, as it had not been in recent centuries. A question,
unlike an assumption embedded in rhetorical convention,
generates models and hypotheses, as well as antithetical
pairs of positions, each of which implies the other.

Making the natural order a question produced an immense variety of Mid-Tang landscapes, a variety that does not

---

[3] This aspect of rhetorical mechanism in classical poetry was even
stronger and more explicit in poetic expositions, *fu* 賦, where the representation is usually presented as impersonal rather than experiential.
For the link between cosmology and rhetoric, see my *Traditional Chinese
Poetry and Poetics: An Omen of the World* (Madison: University of Wisconsin Press, 1985), pp. 78–107.

permit any simple generalization. One particularly important pair of antithetical positions, however, can be found in the passages cited above. At one extreme, the medieval order may be made explicit, with Nature represented as architectural, purposefully structured, luminously intelligible, and with each part contributing to the whole. The antithetical position is already presumed in the very need to explicitly assert architectural unity in Nature. In this antithetical version Nature is an aggregation of details, either lacking unifying order altogether or suggesting a hidden and unintelligible order. Facing architectural Nature, the human subject stands at a distance, recognizing the whole in sweeping vistas; set amid fragmentary Nature, the human subject becomes disoriented and absorbed in the particular.

The architectural landscape usually consists of symmetries, a center that defines motion and limits symmetry, and a core plot that organizes space experientially (such as movement through the landscape as progress to enlightenment or knowledge). The architectural landscape is totalizing and microcosmic; that is, its validity is guaranteed by its ability to subsume all particulars and integrate them as components of the whole or fractal reproductions of the whole, and the totality of the limited space represented structurally duplicates the totality of all natural space. In the architectural landscape the subject always "knows where he stands."

Han Yu's "South Mountains" is a spectacular example of such an architectural representation, in which each descriptive element finds a place in the transparent order of the whole. "South Mountains" is a very long poem, involving complex symmetries, a generative center, and an enlightenment narrative that culminates in the reproduction of Nature's order in the textual representation.[4] In the closing summation of the following passage, Han Yu praises the purposeful order

---

[4] For an extensive discussion of "South Mountains," see Stephen Owen, *The Poetry of Meng Chiao and Han Yü* (New Haven: Yale University Press, 1975), pp. 198–209.

of the universe and, as the human witness, reverentially acknowledges the creator with the offering of the intricate text
as counterpart of and recompense for the intricate world:[5]

大哉立天地，經紀肖營膜。
厥初孰開張，僶俛誰勸侑。
創茲樸而巧，戮力忍勞疚。
得非施斧斤，無乃假詛咒。
鴻荒竟無傳，功大莫酬僦。
嘗聞於祠官，芬苾降歆臭。
斐然作歌詩，惟用贊報有。

Mighty they stand between Heaven and Earth,
in orderly function like the body's ducts and
   veins.
Who was he who first laid out their origin?
Who, in labor and striving, urged it on?
Creating in this place the simple and artificed,
with forces joined, he bore long-suffering toil.
Could he have not applied hatchet and ax?—
he must have used spells and incantations.
No tradition survives from the Age of Chaos,
such a mighty deed none can repay.
I have heard from the priest in charge of
   sacrifice
that he descends to taste the offering's sweet
   scent.
Finely wrought, I made this poem,
by which I may join in requiting him.

This is a fascinating passage, beginning with the comparison
of the mountains to a living body, and moving immediately to
the body's creator. Since the impersonal, creator-less physics
of medieval Chinese cosmology would have produced the very
symmetrical order that Han Yu has discovered in the moun-

----

[5] I would like to bracket the serious questions that surround the
use of the term "creator." Although this is clearly not the Judeo-
Christian deity that makes the universe from nothing by *logos* (in fact,
Han Yu is quite explicit about the hard work involved), the term is still
worth retaining to distinguish this intentionally constructed version of
Nature from Nature as pure mechanism.

tains, we may well wonder what prompted him to construct the fiction of a creator here. Often in Mid-Tang writing we find hypotheses that link order and purposiveness, with the human subject standing as the ultimate recipient of purposive order. Instead of being an integral part of the natural order, which was the medieval assumption, the human subject is thrown into a relation with this purposive intelligence—an intelligence, I might add, that turns out to be ruthless and cruel as often as it is benign. The physical universe, either shaped or informed by such purposive intelligence, becomes the mere medium by which the intelligence is known and the subject affected.

Such a radical shift from an impersonal cosmological mechanism to Nature informed by purposeful intelligence had little basis in the Chinese tradition. Perhaps as a result, representations of purposeful Nature tend to be hypotheses, poetic fictions, or simply tongue-in-cheek. Texts in which the case is posed in a serious way (as sometimes occurs in Meng Jiao and Li He) may carry a strong suggestion of a passion akin to madness.

Han Yu's awed appreciation of the creator's achievements is a poetic move, or at most a religious impulse; it is not a religious conviction. The creator is conveniently displaced into the remote past, and his deeds can only be inferred from the perfection of the product—a potentially more compelling authority is avoided by a break in the textual tradition ("no tradition survives from the Age of Chaos").[6]

Han Yu's poem serves several functions. It fills the gap left by the broken textual tradition. It contributes to a balancing of accounts by its recognition of and reward for service done (unwittingly calling up the image of Han Yu as emperor or member of the literary elite acknowledging the services of the god as artisan and manual laborer). Finally, in producing

---

[6] This echoes a passage early in the poem (ll. 5–10) in which Han Yu considers earlier texts about South Mountains and rejects them as inadequate, deciding to observe the mountains himself.

his finely wrought miniature representation of the landscape, Han Yu places himself in a position corresponding to that of the creative divinity; Han Yu is himself the purposeful intelligence behind this second creation that is the poem.

"South Mountains" is cosmic and imperial, with all particulars, in their immense variety, finding their place in the orderly whole. This local landscape south of Chang'an is a microcosm, less a particular place than a model of all imperial space. The poem's vision of the natural order is glorious but unproblematic, and it is a useful foil for reading a very different representation of Nature as a mass of fragments. In the fragmentary landscape, artfully constructed particulars are discovered *against* the coherence of the whole. Here the engrossing pleasure of the detail resists integration into a totality.

In Li He's "Changgu," Nature seems to offer an overabundance of fascinating details, which absorb the poet's attention. There are brief moments that orient his motion through the landscape—a road, some landmarks, a shift from mountain forests to agricultural land—but these signposts of organized space serve primarily as points from which to repeat the experience of disorientation, of being swallowed up in the marvels of the particular. Attention swings wildly in direction and scale, and in the beautiful patterns that arrest attention, Nature's marvels are indistinguishable from the ingenuity of poetic craft.[7]

---

[7] "Changgu" of 811 was strongly influenced by Meng Jiao and Han Yu's "South of the City Linked Verse," "Chengnan lianju," of 806. There are strong similarities in the style of the descriptive couplets and numerous particular echoes of unusual usages. On a deeper level, Li He is re-creating the peculiar aesthetic pleasure of that unique linked verse. As in all linked verses, "South of the City" is based on the serial responses of the participants, which makes architectural unity impossible. "South of the City" was, however, also a formal experiment, different from other linked verses in being based on capping lines to form parallel couplets. This placed a special premium on both poetic ingenuity, realized in the marvelous details observed, and on discontinuity, since the first line of each couplet was posed as a challenge. Li He saw the aes-

昌谷五月稻，細青滿平水。遙巒相壓疊，頹綠愁墮地。
光潔無秋思，涼曠吹浮媚。竹香滿淒寂，粉節塗生翠。
草髮垂恨鬒，光露泣幽淚。層圍爛洞曲，芳徑老紅醉。
攢蟲鎪古柳，蟬子鳴高邃。大帶委黃葛，紫繷交狹浹。
石錢差復籍，厚葉皆蟠膩。汰沙好平白，立馬印青字。
晚鱗自遨遊，瘦鵠暝單峙。嘹嘹濕蛄聲，咽源驚濺起。
紆緩玉眞道，神娥蕙花裹。苔絮縈澗礫，山實垂禎紫。
小柏儼重扇，肥松突丹髓。鳴流走響韻，壠秋拖光穟。
鶯唱閔女歌，瀑懸楚練帔。風露滿笑眼，駢繷雜舒墜。
亂篠进石嶺，細頸喧島嘴。日腳掃昏翳，新雲啓華閟。
謐謐厭夏光，商風道清氣。高眠服玉容，燒桂祀天几。
霧衣夜披拂，眠堂夢眞粹。待駕棲鸞老，故宮椒壁圮。
鴻瓏數鈴響，羈臣發涼思。陰藤束朱鍵，龍仗著魑魅。
碧錦帖花椹，香衾事殘貴。歌塵蠹木在，舞綵長雲似。
珍壤割繡段，里俗祖風義。鄰凶不相杵，疫病無邪祀。
飴皮識仁惠，丱角知酖恥。縣省司刑官，戶曹訴租吏。
竹藪添墮簡，石磯引鈎餌。溪灣轉水帶，芭蕉傾蜀紙。
岑光晃毅襟，孤景拂繁事。泉樽陶宰酒，月眉謝郎妓。
丁丁幽鐘遠，矯矯單飛至。霞巘殷嵯峨，危溜聲爭次。
淡蛾流平碧，薄月眇陰悴。涼光入澗岸，廓盡山中意。
漁童下宵網，霜禽竦煙翅。潭鏡滑蛟涎，浮珠噞魚戲。
風桐瑤匣瑟，螢星錦城使。柳綴長縹帶，篁掉短笛吹。
石根緣綠蘚，蘆筍抽丹漬。漂旋弄天影，古檜拿雲臂。
愁月薇帳紅，罥雲香蔓刺。芒麥平百井，閒乘列千肆。
刺促成紀人，好學鴟夷子。

Changgu's midsummer rice paddies,
a fine green fills level waters.
Far-off ridges press in layer on layer,
I worry lest the collapsing verdure fall.
Luminous, pure, no thoughts of the autumn,
cool and spacious, where drifting charms blow.
The scent of bamboo fills lonely stillness,
powdered joints daubed with living azure.

---

thetic possibilities of the form and made something distinctive out of them. Just as Li He used this form to write on his home region, Du Mu, a few decades later, used it again in "Vermilion Bank" 朱坡 to write on his ancestral estate.

The hairs of plants dangle reproachful tresses,
as luminous dew sheds secret tears.
Surrounded in tiers, a shimmering tunnel's
    curve,
on perfumed paths, the aging reds are drunk.[8]
Swarming insects engrave ancient willows,
cicadas sing out in high, sequestered spots.
In great sashes the yellow *ge* vines trail,
lavender rushes crisscross narrow shores.
Stone coins of moss in disarray dispersed,
thick leaves all coiling and glossy.
Washed sands nicely white and flat,
the standing horse imprints green characters.
Evening fins roam carefree,
a gaunt heron in darkness singly poised.
Cheeping, the damp mole-crickets' voices,
from gurgling springs the startled splashings
    rise.
The Jade Being's road winds in tortuous turns,
the goddess maid is among the orchids.
Streamers of moss entwine brook pebbles,
mountain fruits dangle maroon and purple.
Small cypress are just like tiers of fans,
plump pines spurt cinnabar marrow.
The sounding streams speed resonant echoes,
autumn on slopes trails luminous ears of grain.
Orioles perform the Min girls' songs,
cascades hang frocks of white Chu silk.
Windy dew is filled with smiling eyes,
ranged cliffs where unfurling and falling mix.
Tangled bamboo burst from stony crags,
thin throats make noise on purling isles.
Sunbeams sweep away the dusky shadows,
new clouds disclose their flowery recesses.
When balmy calm wearies of summer's light,
fall winds will usher in clear air.

[8] I.e., blossoms.

Sleeping on high, the face that swallowed jade,
cassia burns in prayer at the heavenly altar.
Her fog-like robes by night flutter in breeze,
in the sleeping hall, dreams of pure beings.
Awaiting the coach, the roosting simurgh ages,
an ancient palace, its pepper-scented walls in
ruin.
Tingling, several echoes of bells
bring cool thoughts to the officer traveling.
Shadowy vines bind vermilion door-bolts,
dragon drapes touch kobolds and imps.
Sapphire brocades stuck with flowering
tamarisk,
scented quilts served the vanished nobles.
Of song's dust only worm-eaten wood remains,
of the dancers' silks, long clouds are the
semblance.
Treasured terrain, hacked patches of brocade,
local customs revere manners and the right.
Neighbor's affliction leaves no pestle pounding,[9]
in times of plague, no dark witchery.
Mottled-skinned elders meet with kindness and
grace,
while tufted children blush and know shame.
The county has reduced officers of punishment,
households lack clerks cursing them for taxes.
Bamboo thickets add fallen slips for writing,
stone jetties lure the hooked bait.
Stream coves turn their liquid sashes,
plantains dip Shu's paper down to me.
Light from peaks glows on crepe lapels,
lonely rays brush off all thronging cares.
My spring-filled goblet, Warden Tao's wine;
the moon's brow, Master Xie's dancing girl.[10]
Ding-dong, a bell unseen afar

---

[9] According to the *Classic of Rites*, mortars were not to be used
when a neighbor died.
[10] "Warden Tao" is Tao Qian. "Master Xie" is Xie An.

and soaring high, a single flier comes.
Wispy summits, rust-red, towering,
precipitous spillage with sounds racing.
The pale moth drifts in level sapphire,[11]
moon lightly veiled, faint in the shadowy gloom.
As its cool rays enter the torrent's banks,
to the limit my mood in the hills expands.
The fisher lad lets down his nets by night,
and frosty fowl shoot up on misty wings.
The pool mirror slick with kraken froth,
pearls adrift where bubbling fish make sport.
Wind in the tong tree, zither in onyx case,
firefly stars, legates to Brocade City.[12]
Willows compose long turquoise sashes,
bamboo quiver their short flutes piping.
Roots of the rocks follow green lichens,
reed shoots sprout from cinnabar ooze.
Swirling eddies play with the sky's reflections,
ancient junipers clasp the arms of cloud.
Saddening moonlight, curtains of roses red,
snaring clouds, the thorns of scented vines.
Bearded grain lies level past a hundred wells,
idle coaches line a thousand shops.
Put to hard tasks, the man of Chengji
would do well to emulate Master Winesack.[13]

If Han Yu's "South Mountains" has the organic unity of a
normative body, then Changgu's forests, described in the first

[11] The "pale moth" could conceivably be literal, but more likely refers to a brow, which in turn would be the moon. "Moth," *e* 蛾, could also
be Chang E, the moon goddess. A literal moth is tempting because of a
line by Han Yu from "South of the City," describing a ruined estate:
"White moths fly over the dance grounds."

[12] A certain Li Ge in the Han knew that emissaries were on their
way from the Han court to Chengdu ("Brocade City") because he saw two
shooting stars. Li He seems to be playfully comparing the fireflies to
these.

[13] The "man of Chengji" is Li Guang, the Han general, from whom Li
He claimed descent. "Master Winesack" is Fan Li, the advisor of Yue,
who gave up his post and set off to sail the lakes of central China.

half of the poem, are strewn with fragments of woman's body. This landscape clearly has no architectural unity: there is a road to the temple of the goddess Jade Being, then later the temple of the goddess herself, which quickly fades into a ruined palace. But the poet can never see the whole of this forest landscape; it engulfs him with mysterious and isolated presences. The second half of the poem begins by attempting to counterbalance this engulfing maternal landscape with a patriarchal agrarian landscape, initially observed in a vista of orderly field patterns, but soon this idyllic space is itself transformed into absorbing fragments.

It is significant that this impossibly dense, virtually unreadable poem represents the landscape of Li's home region. It is a space without architectural order because one cannot see it perfectly from the outside; stability of perspective is missing. At the end Li tries to pull back to a final vista and a judgment, but a look at the preceding couplets shows that it is a forced move, tearing Li's attention away from curtains of roses and cloud-snaring vines. The only other movement to a vista occurs at the abrupt transition from the feminized forest of the goddess to the scene of orderly fields and a virtuous agrarian society. This transition turns upon a remarkable sequence of images: the gowns of vanished dancers are echoed in the colored clouds; then fabric suddenly becomes "hacked patches of brocade" forming the pattern of fields. Orderly structure is achieved by violently rending more fluid shapes. After a few lines in praise of local customs, Li returns to his absorption in intricate couplets; the poet becomes again the child crawling over a vast embroidery, focusing on the finely wrought details in the folds. Each remarkable detail echoes the quality of the place, whether the feminine presence of the goddess throughout the forest or the pastoral ease of the patriarchal farmland. Those details, however, are essentially discontinunous. Nor can we decide whether those remarkable details are the magic of the place or the poet's craft.[14]

---

[14] For the anecdotal link between the engulfing maternal presence, the landscape of Li He's home region, and the composition of discontinuous lines and couplets, see pp. 110–12.

The aesthetic appeal of the extended fragmentary landscape may be related to the transformations occurring in
early ninth-century regulated verse, represented by poets
such as Jia Dao, Yao He, and others. In the decades that followed, this new aesthetic would be developed by Xu Hun,
Yong Tao, and many more. In these eight-line poems, brilliant
parallel couplets in the middle are often set off by what often
seem to be willfully flat opening and closing couplets. The
parallel couplet becomes a jewel in a setting, calling attention
to itself and to its distinction from, rather than integration
with, the poem as a whole. The very beauty of the couplet *resists* integration. Such poems were often occasional poems,
and as such they situated the poetic act in a larger sphere of
social life; the poem as a whole was supposed to represent
lived experience and feeling. By directing attention away from
the poem as a whole to the artistry of the perfect couplet
(which was often composed independently), the poet called
attention to himself as craftsman rather than as social being.
Formally and socially this was a means of "setting apart"—
distinguishing the true poet from general humanity, using the
focus of attention in a triumph of craft to break the cultural
drive toward normative structures of unity.

In regulated verse such play of the part against the whole
is relatively straightforward. In long landscape poems such as
"Changgu," artful couplets are aggregated until they become
disorienting, almost oppressive.[15] One cannot gain perspective on this space (as Han Yu does in "South Mountains") and
reduce its particulars to illustrations of an integrated universal order. The South Mountains are the microcosm of the
universe; Changgu is a particular place, not like others. In
the judgment of many traditional critics, "South Mountains"
is one of the greatest poems in the language; Li He's
"Changgu" is tedious and seriously flawed as a whole. But by

---

[15] Such landscapes owe something to the older descriptive *pailü*
排律, long, regulated poems, but *pailü* usually kept such couplets in
control by a strict rhetorical order.

themselves Li He's lines and couplets give pleasure and bear scrutiny more than any line or couplet in "South Mountains."

The architectural and the willfully fragmentary versions of natural order, the centripetal and the centrifugal forces, appear in history almost simultaneously (keep in mind that both "South of the City Linked Verse," the model for "Changgu," and "South Mountains" were written at about the same time in 806). Each term of the antithesis is capable of generating the other; we cannot say which came first. We could say that the explicit assertion of totalizing order compensated for fascination with the particular, or we could say that the fascination with the particular was a reaction to an increasingly explicit discourse of totalization. We do know, however, that both terms of the antithesis were alien to the medieval order that dominated discourse earlier, in the eighth century. Medieval discourse assumed universal order, but it left order on the level of an assumption and did not rigorously demand that each particular have its place. In "South Mountains" Han Yu interprets as he describes, and description supports the interpretation. In "Changgu" Li He makes occasional gestures of explicit interpretation, but these are swallowed up by the patterns in the details.

By the Mid-Tang we are already on our way to the familiar Neo-Confucian world of late imperial China, where explicit assertions of a natural and moral order are constituted against a seething subsurface that hungers for absorption in the particular and in the moment—whether in sensuality, in violence, or even in art. This antithesis helps to explain the peculiar hostility of many moralist critics toward the craft of the couplet. Such disapproval is deeper than the mere objection to frivolity, the couplet as a waste of time that might be spent on more uplifting pursuits. Poetic craft was seen to be somehow opposed to poetry's role in the larger civilizing mission of Confucian culture. The High Tang couplet, with its rhetorical basis grounded in cosmological principles, seemed to reinforce order. But the Mid- and Late Tang poet tended to look for and construct "marvels," *qi* 奇, the artful and irreducible particular, analogies based on ingenuity or mystery. The pleasure such couplets gave was absorbing, directed away from larger issues and constituted *against* them.

Our antithetical pair, the totalizing architectural representation of the natural order and the aggregation of absorbing fragments that refuse integration, circumscribes a realm of possibility without accounting for what can occur between the extremes. The issue is raised: Do we inhabit a world that is constructed and explicable, or do we inhabit a world of mystery and irreducible marvels? Does some god or purposeful intelligence lie at the heart of the landscape and the natural world?

> From the point where West Mountain road comes out, I went straight north, crossing over Yellow Reed Ridge and coming down the other side. There I found two roads. One went off to the west; I followed it, but found nothing. The other went north a bit and then turned to the east, where, after no more than a hundred and twenty-five yards, the dry land stopped at the fork of a river. There a mass of rock lay stretched across the margin. Along the top were the shapes of battlements and timbers, while to the side were palisades and a keep, which had something like a gateway in it. When I peered inside, it was completely black. I tossed a stone in, and there was a splash of water in a cavernous space. The echoes continued to resound for a long time. By circling around I could climb to the summit, where I gazed far into the distance. There was no soil, yet fine trees and lovely shafts of bamboo grew there, sturdy and quite unusual. The way they were spread out in clumps and open spaces, together with the angles at which they were set, made it seem like they had been placed there by some intelligence.
>
> For a long time now I have wondered whether there was a creator or not. When I came to this spot, I became even more convinced of his existence. But then I thought it peculiar that he did not make this in the heartland, but instead set it out here in an uncivilized wilderness where, in the passage of centuries and millennia, he could not even once advertise his skill. Thus all his hard labor was to no purpose. Given that a deity should not be like this, perhaps he does not exist after all. Someone said, "It is to provide solace for virtu-

ous men who come to this place in disgrace." Someone else said, "Here the divine forces produce no outstanding men, but instead produce only these things, so that south of Chu there are few people and many rocks." I do not believe either claim.[16]

"An Account of Little Stone Ramparts Mountain," 小石城 山記, written during Liu Zongyuan's Yongzhou exile, can also be dated to 806 or shortly thereafter. It offers us a dark and subtle meditation on the natural landscape as a meaningful construct and the possibility of a creator at work behind the landscape. This landscape appears to be quite literally "architectural" and hence purposive; but in the end it may prove to be no more than a random marvel, precisely because of its separation from imperial topography.

Liu Zongyuan begins his account by giving directions. We should keep in mind the incongruity between the level of precision in these directions and the place, Yongzhou, a far outpost of imperial administration located in the middle of the southern wilderness. This is not one of those late imperial guidebooks for tourists and travelers; insofar as writing is a public act, Liu Zongyuan must be presuming an audience in the northern heartland. Even his fellow exiles of the Wang Shuwen faction will probably not come to Yongzhou, and some may not even see his account until they return to the heartland. Liu Zongyuan is giving precise directions without the expectation that they will ever be used as directions. Even in representations of the topography of regions more likely to be visited and explored, writers at this time did not usually "give directions," as Liu Zongyuan does here and elsewhere in the "Eight Accounts of Yongzhou," 永州八記. What, then, is he doing? Liu is mapping an imaginative space for others, making its exotic novelty intimate, creating an intelligible topographic order in the wilderness. A reader in Chang'an may have had only the vaguest notion of Yongzhou's location, but

[16] Liu Zongyuan, *Liu Zongyuan ji* 柳宗元集 (Beijing: Zhonghua shuju, 1979), pp. 772–73.

Liu Zongyuan's account will allow him to orient Little Stone Ramparts Mountain in relation to other sites around Yongzhou. By creating a small island of the familiar in the middle of the wilderness, Liu Zongyuan anticipates the question he will raise later in the account.

The mention of the road that leads west is of particular interest because this road yields nothing of interest. Why, then, include it at all? No doubt hundreds of other details went unmentioned, but Liu Zongyuan chose to record for us a wrong turn. The comment on the road west is the formal mimesis of giving directions: it can serve no other purpose. The road to the west goes off into blank space, an absence: it is the margin of wilderness. Questions of order and orientation are of primary importance here: they are the antithesis of wilderness. The term Liu Zongyuan uses for this tentative journey into absence is a simple word, but one with immense resonance in the poetics of the period: when he went west, *wu suo de* 無所得, he "found nothing," literally "nothing was gotten." "Getting something," *de* 得, and writing are very closely related (*de* is the word used when one manages to write a couplet or a poem in a given circumstance). To make space intelligible, you have to "get something," *de*, and getting something requires that it have words or a name; that is the only way we can orient one place in relation to another and explain the route to follow. Yongzhou's West Mountain and Yellow Reed Ridge will obviously be unknown to readers in the capital, but relating them to one another is the formal imitation of topography with names. "Name," *ming* 名, in this context has a special meaning: these are not *mingshan* 名山, "famous mountains" or "mountains with names," which identify known reference points on the imaginary map of China. West Mountain and Yellow Reed Ridge, however, are names in a militantly local topography, known only to someone in Yongzhou.

There is another road, a fruitful road that leads north, then east. This road breaks off abruptly at the fork of a river. We note that Little Stone Ramparts Mountain is not something discovered completely by chance along the way; it is a terminus; the road leads there, then stops. Liu Zongyuan represents it as a discovery, *de*; but the road leads him there, and he uses the name "Little Stone Ramparts" as if it were given. Perhaps Liu Zongyuan has named the mountain himself; perhaps it was a local site that he knew about and that was the unacknowledged goal of his journey. All we know from the text is that he came upon it as if by accident and it has a name. The named mountain extends intelligible space; this is not the pure wilderness of the road that led west.

Naming something requires distinction, the ability to recognize a place and distinguish it from others. Wilderness is, by definition, undifferentiated. Distinction, the act that makes the mountain namable, here comes through resemblance, through metaphor: the mountain resembles a city wall (here we might contrast Gumu Hill, whose identifying resemblances were to animals). The similitude gives merely the illusion of purposive and identifiable form. In form, the rocks may look like a city wall, but that is not enough in itself to guarantee purposive order. When, however, Liu Zongyuan considers the deployment of bamboo, the non-mimetic aesthetic order that is organized for experience (like that he himself created in partially clearing Gumu Hill), Liu suspects that in this place Nature has been organized by mind, "some intelligence," *shizhe* 識者. Gross similarity to the artifactual does not prove that Nature imitates art; the proof comes in a shared sense of pattern.

This brings Liu Zongyuan to the wonderful meditation on the creator, whose existence at first seems verified by the intuition of purposive organization. The premises of the immediate countermove are fascinating: the handiwork of the creator, which at first seems to unite the intelligible order of this particular spot with the rest of the world, suddenly is judged impossible precisely because of the surrounding wilderness, by the fact that a local, apparently purposive order is not linked to the order of the whole. Purposive order, making possible attribution or ownership, is predicated on display, on its being recognized. If this particular landscape were the purposive construction of a Creator, it would be *shou qi ji* 售其伎, "selling one's skills" or "advertising one's skills," requiring an audience for its fulfillment. This particular display of craft could be purposive only if there were a civilized audience to recognize it; the site of this potential display calls that possibility into question. Note that this mountain specifically resembles a city wall, the mark of heartland civilization. If we presume a wilderness without walled cities, how can uncivilized natives recognize a feature that has identity only through its resemblance to a walled city, that is, to heartland civilization? Liu Zongyuan clearly does not feel that his own singular visit would have merited the Creator's trouble.

Little Stone Ramparts Mountain can only be a mock fortress in the wilderness, a fortuitous resemblance rather than an imitation. Name is predicated on order, and order is predicated on the possibility of recognition. Ultimately order can only be display. Liu thus concludes that a divinity "ought not to be like this," *bu yi ru shi* 不宜如是. From this Liu hypothesizes the absence of divinity, both in the formation of Little Stone Ramparts Mountain and in the universe. This conclusion gives us an intuition of why Liu Zongyuan's account takes the form it does: it is literary display, constructing the territory around Yongzhou as intelligible topography in an account for others, but a topography that can have meaning only through a particular person's experience of it.

Liu Zongyuan's account concludes with two mock explanations offered by others, each of which suggests an interpretation why such an apparently purposeful structure of Nature should be found in the midst of a wilderness. The first explanation addresses Liu Zongyuan's own situation: this marvel has been placed here for his particular consolation rather than for some general appreciation by people in the heartland. This explanation attributes too much purposiveness to a creator to be believable; such foresight and tender concern can only be a polite fiction. The second explanation, that remarkable rocks are the wilderness's counterpart of remarkable people in the heartland, is hardly a consolation, since it presumes the production of wonders as a mere mechanism working with local materials, without purpose or meaning. Liu cites both explanations to reject them. We are left at last with unintelligible Nature, whose apparent marvels are accidental configurations.[17]

I have neglected to mention one key passage in Liu Zongyuan's account of Little Stone Ramparts Mountain. Liu observes "something like a gateway" in the mountain. This is the doorway that would lead inside the simulacrum of a city wall, an "inside" that would be the purpose of a human construction. Liu goes to that "gate" and peers into a blackness within. He then throws a stone into the core of this artifice, and there is a splash, *dongran* 洞然, the echo of a cavernous emptiness at the heart of the mimetic shape.

At the center of South Mountains and the poem "South Mountains," Han Yu comes to a tarn, which is the home of the dragon, the source of transformations. The beast is invisible, just as the creator is at the end of the poem. Nevertheless its central place has the marks of holiness.

因緣窺其湫，凝湛閟陰獸。
魚蝦可俯掇，神物安敢寇。
林柯有脫葉，欲墮鳥驚救。
爭銜彎環飛，投棄急哺鷇。

Thereby I peered into the tarn,
unmoving and deep, it hides a dark beast.
I could reach now and grab the fish and shrimp,
but who would dare rob the holy creature?
From boughs in the forest leaves are shed,
birds leap to catch any that might fall in.
All take them in beaks, wheeling in flight,
then let them drop as they rush to feed chicks.

---

[17] The rise of the idea of "Natural beauty" in the West originated in the idea of purposiveness associated with a divine creator and was closely tied to the intuition of purposiveness in works of art. These are central issues in Kant's *Critique of Judgment*.

One could not choose a more telling contrast with "An Account of Little Stone Ramparts Mountain": in the center of Liu Zongyuan's mountain, located in the wilderness rather than in the imperial center, there is also a pool, but it is empty and hollow. South Mountains is a legible landscape, a landscape with cause, center, and meaningful symmetry. Little Stone Ramparts Mountain is an accidental resemblance, the mockery of purposive order.

❖

Interpreting

Before the turn of the ninth century, interpretations of natural and social phenomena within Tang literary texts tended to be based on the reformulation and elaboration of received knowledge. Received knowledge on a given topic was not, however, necessarily unified. Someone wishing to write a discourse on Heaven, for example, could draw on a large body of diverse opinion. For a large topic such as Heaven, each of the so-called Three Schools of Learning—Confucians, Daoists, and Buddhists—had not one, but many traditions that offered an authoritative basis on which to develop a position. Conceptual innovation was possible in acts of synthesis and reformulation.[1] This was a discourse of authority, especially textual authority, and such authority was supported by institutional structures.[2] More than anything else, this characteristic of the seventh and eighth centuries, justifies the loosely analogical use of the term "medieval" for the period. If we accept this usage, then the Chinese "middle ages" ended in the Mid-Tang.

Before the Mid-Tang writing had been primarily a public

---

[1] I avoid the term "originality" here, reserving it only for those cases in which an act of innovation is inextricable from the particular nature of the innovator.

[2] We should distinguish clearly between a *discourse* of authority and a social or intellectual world that did not change. A discourse of authority is nothing more than the assertion of continuity and stability. Immense changes did, in fact, occur in these centuries, and many positions that seemed authoritative were actually of recent origin.

statement, even in its construction of the private. There had
not yet developed a sphere of private life from which a person
could make claims and espouse values that would be held
separate from judgments regarding that person's adherence
to public values. A medieval celebration of the joys of with-
drawal to private life could immediately be read as a criticism
of the government; no such suspicion arises when a Mid-Tang
writer like Bai Juyi proclaims his domestic contentment.

The appearance of interpretations strongly marked as *individual* is one of the most striking characteristics of Mid-
Tang writing. Related to this is the tendency to offer an interpretation when none would have been called for earlier. We
might compare parallel moments in European intellectual
history, when challenges were launched against the received
textual authority of the Church and Aristotelian learning during the European Renaissance and Reformation. In those
cases opposition to textual authority was supported by the
assertion of new loci of authority: in empirical observation, in
reason, or in a God who speaks directly to the human heart.
Although these various moves were constituted against received textual authority, they were not truly *individual* interpretations. Somewhere between the witty conceits of the sev-
enteenth century and our contemporary world, in which interpretation is individual property requiring acknowledgment
in notes, an idea of marked individual interpretation took
hold in the West.

Explicitly individual interpretations appeared for a brief
period in Mid-Tang China, and they appeared in a very peculiar way: such interpretations used the pure rhetoric of authority without appeal to any authoritative ground. Furthermore, they appeared without the justification of reinterpreta-
tion based on reason and private study and reflection, which
was to become so important in the Song Dynasty.[3] That is,

---

[3] See Steven Van Zoeren, *Poetry and Personality: Reading, Exegesis,
and Hermeneutics in Traditional China* (Stanford: Stanford University
Press, 1991); and Peter Bol, *"This Culture of Ours"* (Stanford: Stanford
University Press, 1992).

Mid-Tang writers often spoke with the unreflective assurance of authoritative interpretation, but without basis in the repertoire of shared, received truths that made such discourse possible. This led to various consequences in the tone of discourse. One was the suggestion of a demonic, threatening, and unintelligible order in the world, the strong whiff of paranoia that we find in the poetry of Meng Jiao and Li He. Another common consequence of individual interpretation was the generation of hypotheses that were either ironic or haunted by the possibility of irony. On the least problematic level we have the playful cleverness of Bai Juyi's poetry, often built around witty interpretations of small occasions. More difficult are a number of texts by Han Yu that offer interpretations for serious situations, interpretations so idiosyncratic that we do not know how to take them. Among the most famous of these is Han Yu's "Text for the Crocodiles" 鱷魚文, in which Han formally banishes the predatory reptiles from his prefecture and from the empire.

> On the present day, this month, this year, Han Yu, Prefect of Chaozhou, depute Qin Ji, Associate Judge in the military administration, to take one sheep and one pig and to cast them into the pool of the Creek of Woe for the crocodiles to eat and then to make the following announcement to them:
>
> When the kings of olden days held the world, they closed off the marshes and mountains, then spread nets and thrust with blades to rid themselves of all insects and serpents and other evil creatures that did harm to the folk. And they cast those creatures out beyond the encircling seas. When the majesty of later kings weakened and they could no longer keep their distant domains, they abandoned the region between the Yangzi and Han to the rude, uncivilized folk of Chu and Yue. Still less did they hold this region of Chaozhou and the territory between the Southern Alps and the sea, ten thousand leagues from the capital. Here the crocodiles have lurked in the waters and brooded upon their eggs. And they felt secure in their place here.
>
> Now a new Son of Heaven has ascended to the Tang throne. Divine and sagely in his wisdom, merciful yet martial, His Majesty has taken under his protection all that lies

beyond the encircling seas and all within the six ends of the earth. Still more under his protection is this land covered by the peregrinations of Great Yu, the nearby lands of ancient Yangzhou, governed by prefects and county magistrates, soil that produces taxes and tribute for the temples of Heaven and Earth and of the dynastic ancestors, and for the worship of the gods. Crocodiles may not live together in the same land as a prefect!

I, the prefect, have received the command of the Son of Heaven to hold this land and govern these folk. Yet the crocodiles glare in their discontent; they have occupied the pools of this creek and eat the livestock of the folk, along with bears, boars, deer, and roebuck, by which they fatten themselves and breed offspring. They have set themselves in opposition to the prefect and contend with him for dominance. And though the prefect is but a weak and feeble man, how could he, just because of crocodiles, permit himself to hang his head and lose heart, to become jittery and evasive, humiliated before the populace and his subordinates in order to get by with just his life here! Having furthermore received the command of the Son of Heaven to come here in his service, the situation is such that he has no choice but to clarify this issue with the crocodiles.

If the crocodiles are possessed of intelligence, let them heed the words of the prefect:

The Great Sea lies to the south of Chao Prefecture. It has room for all things to live and feed there, whether they are as huge as the Leviathan and the Peng Bird or as tiny as shrimp and crabs. If the crocodiles left in the morning, they could reach it by evening. So let me now place this injunction on the crocodiles: before three days are up, let them lead their ilk and betake themselves southward to the Sea to escape the appointed servant of the Son of Heaven. If they are unable to do so in three days, I will give them five days; and if they are unable to do so in five days, I will give them seven days. But if they are not gone in seven days, this means they will never be willing to move; this means that they will not recognize the prefect and heed his words. Alternatively, it may mean that the crocodiles are dull-witted and lacking spiritual intelligence; and though the prefect tells them something, they neither hear nor understand. Whether they are flouting the appointed servant of the Son of Heaven by not heeding what he tells them and refusing to move away from him, or they are dim-witted and lacking intelligence, things that harm the folk and other creatures, in either case they may be killed. In that case the prefect will select skilled underlings, taking strong bows and poisoned arrows to deal with the crocodiles. Nor will they stop until all are killed. Let there be no regrets.[4]

In "Text for the Crocodiles" Han Yu deliberately takes the discourse of moral order in Nature, which was inextricably linked to the moral order of the state, and forces it on a pragmatically unlikely situation.[5] He commands the crocodiles to depart from Chaozhou in the name of the authority delegated to him by the emperor. Then he raises the alternative possibility, that the moral order of the state perhaps cannot be communicated to Nature and the crocodiles may indeed be creatures "lacking spiritual intelligence," *buling* 不靈.[6] He closes with a putative situation in which the decision between the two interpretations cannot be made and need not be made. If the crocodiles do not leave, they are either recalcitrant or unintelligent; in either case they deserve to be killed.

Han Yu's official biography takes pains to tell us that the crocodiles did indeed depart from Chaozhou. This conclusion is driven by the cultural necessity to affirm the moral authority of the state in Nature. This anecdotal supplement provides the only outcome that does not leave this important question undecided and undecidable. At the same time, however, the information that the crocodiles did indeed leave Chaozhou takes us into the realm of *qi* 奇, the "unusual" or "remark-

[4] Ma Qichang 馬其昶, ed., *Han Changli wenji jiaozhu* 韓昌黎文集校注 (Shanghai: Zhonghua shuju, 1964), pp. 330–31.

[5] We should also note that as in the "Memorial on the Buddha's Bone" or the "Letter in Reply to Li Yi," "Text for the Crocodiles" asserts claim to something by exclusions, getting rid of what is alien and not "proper" to it.

[6] *Ling* 靈 is the quality of "divinity," but is also the quality of intelligence in creatures; thus the *Shu* says that "man is, of all creatures, the one most possessed of spiritual intelligence," *wei ren wanwu zhi ling* 惟人萬物之靈.

able"; that is, it was worth recording only because it was the *unexpected* consequence of Han Yu's declaration. By formulating the question so that it would remain undecided, Han Yu had also managed to keep it within the realm of the normative.

Let me reiterate: if the crocodiles do not depart, they are either unintelligent or intelligent and recalcitrant; they will be killed in either case, and one cannot decide between the two interpretive possibilities. I would strongly suggest that the crocodiles did *not* leave Chaozhou and that Han Yu did not expect them to leave. The anecdote that has them leave is the only way to reaffirm intelligibility in a situation Han Yu has created, a situation that willfully (and perhaps wittily) calls the intelligibility of Nature into question. It is not enough to reduce the possibilities to the two versions of Heaven proposed at the beginning of Liu Yuxi's "Discourse on Heaven" 天論: Heaven (Nature) as purposive moral order and Heaven as mindless mechanism. There is also a profound incongruity in applying a "high" intellectual issue to the crocodiles, an incongruity that threatens to make the question ironic and undermine it.[7] Such large issues were supposed to apply to all things, but Mid-Tang writers well understood the comic potential in a conflict between ideological universalizing and common sense.

Han Yu has taken a contemporary intellectual issue and played with it in writerly fashion, creating within it a set of conflicts and incongruities that make it irreducible to a position. Combined with powerfully authoritative rhetoric, this impulse to a destabilizing play of ideas calls the true inten-

---

[7] Many scholars would take this text as an innocent expression of Han Yu's sense of the Confucian moral order and its role in the natural world. This was a large issue; however, such an interpretation disregards the anomalous nature of this text. Tang prefects did not habitually make formal verbal addresses to the local fauna. The piece is possibly a syncretic response to a local cult, politely accepting the premises of crocodile worship and reformulating man's relation to the crocodiles in Confucian terms. But if so, it is still ironic.

tions of the speaker into question. Han Yu creates the kind of problem that the biographer must resolve by affirming the one outcome, however empirically unlikely, that restores intelligibility to the world and effective purpose to the act of address.

Many of Han Yu's texts are extreme cases of the Mid-Tang impulse to pose an individual interpretation as pure hypothesis, the writer's own construct. Whatever claims on truth he makes explicitly, he can simultaneously disclaim full responsibility for the assertion precisely in offering it only as his own. One of the most remarkable of Han Yu's hypotheses is reported by Liu Zongyuan.[8]

韓愈謂柳子曰，若知天之說乎。吾爲子言天之說。

Han Yu addressed Master Liu, "Do you know the theory about Heaven? Well, I will tell you the theory."

Liu Zongyuan begins the "Theory of Heaven" 天說 abruptly, with Han Yu speaking to him with a certain urgency, an urgency achieved by keeping silent regarding the circumstances that led to this question. Han Yu's question "Do you know" presumes an ignorance on Liu's part. Such a presumption of ignorance is remarkable because we would expect that Liu Zongyuan did indeed know theories of Heaven—as reformulations of common knowledge or opinion. The opening act of address leads us to expect something new here, something hitherto unknown. The very generic term "theory," *shuo* 說, in this period tends to the realm of the singular interpretation. We are therefore justified in translating the opening: "Do you know *my* theory about Heaven? Well, I will tell you *my* theory." Indeed, the "Theory of Heaven" turns out to be a most singular interpretation of man's place in the cosmos.

As with the infestation of crocodiles in Chaozhou or, as we will see later, with Meng Jiao's loss of his son, Han Yu's singular interpretation is offered in response to a crisis, the

[8] Liu Zongyuan, *Liu Zongyuan ji* 柳宗元集 (Beijing: Zhonghua shuju, 1979), pp. 441–43.

apparent failure of the dominant interpretation of Heaven as
a moral order.

> These days whenever someone suffers from the torment of
> disease or is worn down by humiliation or endures hunger
> and cold, he looks up and cries out to Heaven: "Those who
> harm folk flourish; those who help folk perish!" Or they look
> up and cry out to Heaven: "Why have you caused things to
> go so utterly wrong?" No one who behaves like this truly un-
> derstands Heaven.

The easy response to such incomprehensible suffering would
be that it is "ordained," *ming* 命, without reference to the justice or injustice of inscrutable Necessity. Among the writings
of Han Yu's friends and contemporaries, however, we find
representations of an anthropomorphic Heaven, either ruth-
lessly self-serving or indifferent. Han Yu will now demonstrate
that Heaven is a moral order behind this apparent moral inversion.

> When a piece of fruit or a melon has become too rotten to
> eat, insects grow in it. When the vitality of a man's blood
> fails and becomes sluggish, abscesses, swelling pustules,
> and hemorrhoids form; insects grow in these too. When
> wood rots, there are grubs within; when plants putrefy, fire-
> flies come forth from them. These are obviously things that
> appear only after decay sets in. When something decays, in-
> sects are born out of it; when the Primordial Force or Yin
> and Yang decayed, out of that human beings were born.

The comparison of human beings to maggots in rotting
fruit and abscesses or grubs in wood is intentionally shocking
in its violation of the presumed hierarchy in which humankind is the most "numinous" or "spiritually intelligent," *ling*
靈, of all creatures. Han Yu deliberately uses words that
would be considered uncouth in elevated Tang discourse
(though Zhuangzi would have approved). Analogies were often
drawn across hierarchical levels of being, but such a subversion of hierarchy—in which human beings retain their distinction by being the worst in a set of destructive forces—was
rarely exploited.

When insects grow in a thing, it decays even further. Chewing at it, boring holes in it, the harm that the insects inflict on the thing increases greatly. If someone were able to get rid of them, such a person would have done a good deed on behalf of the thing. But whoever lets them multiply and gives comfort to them is the enemy of the thing. The incremental decay that human beings cause to the Primordial Force and to Yin and Yang has also increased greatly. Men plow meadows and fields; they cut down the mountain forests; they dig down to underground springs to find wells that provide them with drink; they excavate graves in which to put their dead. Moreover, they dig latrines; they pound hard earthen walls to surround their homes and their cities; they raise platforms of pounded earth on which to build pavilions and lodges for their excursions; they dig channels for rivers and canals, irrigation ditches, and ponds; they kindle wood for fires; they alter metals by smelting them; they mold pottery and grind and polish stone. Everything in the world looks the worse for wear and nothing can follow its own nature—human beings are responsible for this. Seething in their fury, constantly battering, they assault, destroy, ruin, and wreck; nor have they ever desisted. Is not the harm they inflict on the Primordial Force and upon Yin and Yang even worse than what insects do? In my opinion if one were able to cut away at humanity and make them dwindle over the days and years, then the harm inflicted on the Primordial Force and Yin and Yang would steadily diminish. Whoever could accomplish this would have done a good deed for Heaven and Earth. But whoever lets them multiply and gives comfort to them is the enemy of Heaven and Earth. These days no one understands Heaven, so people cry out to it in reproach. In my opinion, when Heaven hears their cries of reproach, then those who have done it a good deed will inevitably receive a rich reward, but those who have inflicted harm on it will inevitable receive grave punishment. What do you think of what I have said?

Analogies call not so much for proof as amplification in particulars that seem, in their variety, to confirm the analogical proposition. A good analogy inspires the writer to discover such particulars, and here the heretical analogy provokes even more heretical particulars. The destructive force of human beings is revealed precisely in the items that constitute civilization—farming, building cities, burying the dead—the very values that Han Yu normally supports. Liu Zongyuan is correct in seeing here something of a radical Daoist naturalism, but he refuses to see the essential twist that makes this even more radical than Zhuangzi. On one level Zhuangzi remains a humanist. Zhuangzi would read this same evidence as the unfortunate distortion of human nature by civilization, a distortion to be remedied by philosophy. Han Yu takes the side of Heaven and Earth, reading human civilization as a crime to be punished. Heaven does not operate directly here, erasing maggot-sapiens from the face of the earth. Rather it delights in random death or harm to any member of the human species.

Master Liu then said, "Was there something that got you truly worked up that you propose this? It is well argued indeed and beautifully put. But let me carry this theory to its conclusion. The human world refers to what is dark, mysterious, and above us as Heaven; they refer to what is brown and beneath us as Earth. They refer to that vast, undifferentiated murkiness in between as the Primordial Force; and they refer to the cold and heat as Yin and Yang. However large these are, they are no different from fruits and melons, abscesses and pustules, or plants and trees.

"Let us suppose there were someone or something able to get rid of what bores holes in them—would there be any reward for such a creature? Or one that let them multiply and gave them comfort—would there be any anger against such? Heaven and Earth are a large fruit. The Primordial Force is a large pustule. Yin and Yang are a large tree. How could such things reward a good deed or punish harms inflicted? Those who do such good deeds do so on their own; those who inflict harm, inflict it on their own. To expect either reward or punishment is great folly. Those who cry out in reproach, expecting Heaven will feel sorry for them and be kind to them, show even greater folly. As for you, you trust in your own sense of kindness and right and move freely within that, during your life and on until your death—why attribute your

preservation or destruction, your gains and your losses, to a piece of fruit, a pustule, or a tree?"

It is tempting to read Han Yu's theory of Heaven as a brief on behalf of the crocodiles. When Liu Zongyuan reports Han Yu's "theory" that human beings are the corrupting maggots of the natural world and their destruction would benefit Heaven, the abrogation of received wisdom about Heaven is so extreme that we do not quite know how to understand it. Something drives Han's analogical rhetoric to a position so singular that we do not know if he "means it" and what "meaning it" in this case might be. Han Yu has, in effect, preserved the form of a moral order in the universe at the expense of its received content; that is, his hypothesis explains why Heaven's apparent injustice is justice rather than evidence of Heaven's indifference. Han Yu produces a theory that reconciles the assumption (that Heaven is just) and the fact (that Heaven harms people).

We might distinguish between an argument based on categorical correspondences and an argument by analogy. On one level both are analogical arguments; however, an argument based on categorical correspondences appeals to analogies that have become taken for granted, so that they seem to be, in some essential way, "natural," with similar properties shared by things of the same category. Han Yu's argument is merely "analogical" because it is surprising, using the familiar and authoritative form of correspondence but with unexpected content. It is that element of "discovery" through discursive procedures in Han Yu's analogy that permits Liu Zongyuan to say: "well argued indeed and beautifully put," *xin bian qie mei yi* 信辯且美矣. The *bian*, "well argued," is precisely that special capacity to discover fresh conclusions by strict analogical argumentation, but the *mei*, "beautifully put," is interesting. Given the context, this *mei* is clearly not pleasant in the least; but as an argument it is both "attractive" and "beguiling," compelling by its rhetoric and even by the way it works out a problem—although the conclusion is so repugnant it cannot be allowed to stand. Through both the *bian* and the *mei*, Liu Zongyuan is shifting attention away from Han Yu's proposition in its own right to rhetorical persuasiveness in itself.

Liu Zongyuan's initial response to Han Yu's hypothesis is of particular interest: "Was there something that got you truly worked up that you propose this?" With this comment, Liu interprets the interpretation; that is, he explains the theory as a response to some particular personal circumstance and thus limits the truth-claim of the outrageous hypothesis to explain anything more than Han Yu's circumstantial distress. In doing this, Liu undermines the more interesting and problematic quality of Han Yu's theory as being both ironic and "having a truth to it." Han Yu's notion of Nature as morally organized but hostile verges on the unthinkable. Not content with reducing Han Yu's argument to a merely circumstantial response, Liu refines it with the proposal that Heaven is an amoral mechanism, thus bringing it back securely into the thinkable, one version of received wisdom, the Daoist version. Han Yu's theory was constituted precisely to avoid this, to reconcile purposefulness in Nature with the obvious evidence of human suffering. Liu Yuxi's more fully developed "Discourse on Heaven" 天論 is an elaborate attempt to deny the threatening possibility that Han Yu proposes with his theory. The dangerous hypothesis that arose from Han Yu's ability to use the rhetoric of authority without authoritative grounding led to that more "serious" reflection on the issue. But in essence Liu Yuxi's "Discourse on Heaven" is functionally identical to the anecdote that has the crocodiles leave Chaozhou in response to Han Yu's proclamation: it attempts to put to rest a question that has been put into play.

Han Yu's interpretation is individual in the sense that he "comes up with it" and in the sense that it is constituted against received wisdom. When such an interpretation is presented with the confident rhetoric of authority, of which Han Yu was the master ("it is well argued indeed and beautifully put"), the interpretation is potentially made ironic or, in a closely related mode, made merely subjective, as Liu Zong-yuan did by attributing Han Yu's theory to something that upset him.

As suggested earlier, individual interpretation is closely tied to the impulse to offer an interpretation in situations where none had been previously called for (for example, a public explanation why you intend to exterminate the crocodiles in your prefecture). There were social situations that called for normative statements of emotional response: confronting a death, the writer should express his grief, either on his own account or on behalf of the person who suffered the loss. Such norms of response were the individuated performance of ritual. To offer an interpretation of such a situation, however, was something else altogether—namely, the desire to assert reflective control over the situation. When measured against the weight of feeling it attempts to contain, it is always in danger of becoming mere rationalization.

Han Yu, *Meng Jiao (Dongye) Loses His Sons*
孟東野失子 (17881)

東野連產三子，不數日輒失之。幾老，念無後以悲。其友人昌黎
韓愈，懼其傷也，推天假其命以喻之。

Dongye had three sons in succession, but lost each abruptly after only a few days. Since he is getting old, he has become preoccupied with having no posterity and saddened by it. His friend Han Yu of Changli fears he will do himself harm. I have made inferences about Heaven and undertaken a fictive charge in order to make him understand.

失子將何尤，吾將上尤天。女實主下人，與奪一何偏。
彼於女何有，乃令蕃且延。此獨何罪辜，生死旬日間。
上呼吾時聞，滴地淚到泉。地祇爲之悲，瑟縮久不安。
乃呼大靈龜，騎雲款天門。問天主下人，薄厚胡不均。
天曰天地人，由來不相關。吾懸日與月，吾繫星與辰。
日月相噬齧，星辰踏與顛。吾不女之罪，知非女由緣。
且物各有分，孰能使之然。有子與無子，禍福未可原。
魚子滿母腹，一一欲誰憐。細腰不自乳，舉族長孤鰥。
鴟梟啄母腦，母死子始翻。蝮蛇生子時，拆裂腸與肝。

好子雖云好，未還恩與勤。惡子不可說，鴟梟蝮蛇然。
有子且勿喜，無子固勿歎。上聖不待教，賢聞語而遷。
下愚聞語惑，雖教無由悛。大靈頓頭受，即日以命還。
地祇謂大靈，女往告其人。東野夜有夢，有夫玄衣巾。
闖然入其戶，三稱天之言。再拜謝玄夫，收悲以歡忻。

"In losing a son how can one fix blame?—
but I will blame Heaven above.
Truly in your rule of men below
you are too unfair in giving and taking away.
What are those others to you
that you make them flourish and extend?
And what wrong has this man done
that these lives pass in a ten-day span?"
He shouted upward and never was heard,
tears, dripping to earth, reached the streams
    below.
Earth's Spirit was made sad by them—
he shriveled up, long ill at ease.
Then he called to the Great Tortoise Spirit
to ride clouds and knock at Heaven's gate.
It asked Heaven of its rule of men below,
why such imbalance in the gifts it bestowed.
And Heaven said: "Heaven, Earth, and Man
have never had any connection.
I hung the sun and moon above,
I strung the planets and stars;
and if the sun and moon are eclipsed
or if the stars stumble and fall,
I don't make it a crime of yours,
knowing that you are not the cause.
Moreover, each thing has its portion,
and no one makes it to be so.
And as for having sons or not,
who knows if this is fair fortune or foul.
Fish spawn fill their mother's belly—
who could care for each single one?
The thin-waisted wasp does not nurture its own,
all its tribe are ever orphaned and alone.
The owlet pecks out its mother's brains,
the child flies off only when the mother dies.
And when the viper bears its young,

they rip apart her belly and liver.
And however good a son may be,
he never repays the love and care.
A bad son should not be spoken of—
the owl and the viper are thus.
So don't delight in having a son,
and by no means sigh if you lack one.
The highest sage needs no instruction;
wise men hear and change where they stand;
when the dullard hears, he doubts,
though instructed, he cannot reform."
The Great Tortoise accepted this, kowtowing,
on that very day he took the charge back.
Then the Earth Spirit told the Great Tortoise:
"Go, thou, and tell the man."
That night Dongye had a dream
of a man clad in a black turban.
In a rush he entered through the door
and thrice proclaimed Heaven's words.
Meng bowed, thanking the man in black,
he ceased to grieve and was greatly cheered.

How are we to read "Meng Jiao Loses His Sons"? Again
Han Yu has proposed an explicitly hypothetical explanation
that stands in painful dissonance with the accepted norms of
response. It is even more uncomfortable to read in conjunction with the "Theory of Heaven," where those who complain
against Heaven's unfairness (as Meng Jiao does in the beginning) are told they are vermin and their destruction pleases
Heaven. The poem not only embodies authoritative rhetoric
without a basis in received opinion, it figures that particular
contradiction in the fable itself: Heaven begins by disclaiming
any connection between itself and humankind, then proceeds
to make a pronouncement that must be reverently accepted,
as if Heaven did indeed rule men below. The social circumstance of the poem forbids an ironic reading, but here it is
evident that explanation has become rationalization. Indeed,the poem bullies Meng Jiao into good spirits, telling him
that any unwillingness to accept the lesson of Heaven means
that he is a dullard beyond hope of instruction.

In a famous letter Zhang Ji 張籍 (ca. 776–ca. 829) accused Han Yu of an excessive fondness for jesting and wit. This is partially true but fails to grasp the larger context, of which Han Yu's humor was only a part. Han Yu compulsively generated interpretations as constructs, but with little respect for the functional role that received interpretations or norms of response played in Tang society. Han Yu had a genius, and genius is always slightly "off." As Han Yu said at the end of "Fire in the Luhun Mountains" 陸渾山火 (17882), he knew he should stop his tongue, but couldn't help himself.

Han Yu's rationalizations pale, however, beside Meng Jiao's poetic madness, his spinning out of fragments of interpretation to explain the death of his child. He begins with a late frost in spring that kills the buds of an apricot tree. The analogy soon gets away from him.

Meng Jiao, *Apricots Untimely Dead*
杏殤 (20066–74)

杏殤，花乳也。霜剪而落。因悲昔嬰，故作是詩。

Apricots untimely dead were nursling flowers. The frost cut them and they fell, which made me sad about my late infant. Thus I wrote these poems.

I

凍手莫弄珠，弄珠珠易飛。
驚霜莫剪春，剪春無光輝。
零落小花乳，爛斑昔嬰衣。
拾之不盈把，日暮空悲歸。

Let no frozen hands play with these pearls—
play with these pearls, and they easily fall.
Let the shock of frost not cut spring away—
cut spring away, and there is no radiance.
Scattered and fallen, the small nursling flowers,
streaked and spotted, my late infant's robes.
I gather them up, they don't fill my hand,
and I go back at sunset in pointless sadness.

II

地上空拾星，枝上不見花。
哀哀孤老人，戚戚無子家。

豈若沒水鳧，不如捨巢鴉。
浪轂破便驚，飛雛裊相誇。
芳嬰不復生，向物空悲嗟。

I pointlessly pick up stars on the ground,
on the branches I see no flowers.
Filled with lament, a lone aging man,
dismal, the home without children.
Better the ducks that sink in the waters,
better the crows forsaking the nest.
Duckling in waves, breaks through, then flies;
fledglings in flight, spiraling, vaunting.
But infant fragrance will live no more,
and facing these creature I helplessly sigh.

III

應是一線淚，入此春木心。
枝枝不成花，片片落剪金。
春壽何可長，霜哀亦已深。
常時洗芳泉，此日洗淚襟。

It must have been that single thread of tears
that entered the heart of this springtime tree.
On branch after branch no flowers formed,
to the cutting metal they fell, piece by piece.
how can spring's long span be lengthened?—
and this frost-lament already grows deep.
In usual times I bathe in streams of blossoms,
but this day I am bathed in tears on my clothes.

IV

兒生月不明，兒死月始光。
兒月兩相奪，兒命果不長。
如何此英英，亦爲弔蒼蒼。
甘爲墮地塵，不爲末世芳。

When my son was born, the moon was not
　　bright;
when my son died, the moon first gave light.
My son and the moon stole each other away,
and thus my son's life could not last long.
But how is it that these blossoms
also bring lament to the gray heavens?

They willingly fell to the dust of earth
and did not make fragrance for posterity.

V

踏地恐土痛，損彼芳樹根。
此誠天不知，剪棄我子孫。
垂枝有千落，芳命無一存。
誰謂生人家，春色不入門。

When I tread the earth, I feared hurting the
    ground,
damaging roots of this blossoming tree.
Heaven did not know this sincerity
and cut away my own descendants.
From drooping branches a thousand fell,
of the blossoms' fates not one survives.
Who says that in homes of the living
spring's beauty does not enter their gates?

VI

冽冽霜殺春，枝枝疑纖刀。
木心既零落，山竅空呼號。
班班落地英，點點如明膏。
始知天地間，萬物皆不牢。

Biting chill, the frost killed spring,
on every branch it seemed a thin knife.
Since the tree's heartwood is stripped and fallen,
holes in the hills howl in vain.
Sparkling blossoms that fell to earth,
speck after speck, like bright spots of oil.
Now I know that between Earth and Sky
all things that exist are frail.

VII

哭此不成春，淚痕三四班。
失芳蝶既狂，失子老亦孱。
且無生生力，自有死死顏。
靈鳳不銜訴，誰爲扣天關。

I weep over how these form no spring,
tracks of tears, three or four streaks.
Losing the blossoms, the butterfly's gone mad,
losing his child, the old man too grows frail.

And lacking that force that breeds life from life,
I have the face that breeds death from death.
The holy phoenix won't carry my suit—
who will knock at Heaven's gates for me?

VIII

此兒自見災，花發多不諧。
窮老收碎心，永夜抱破懷。
聲死更何言，意死不必啡。
病叟無子孫，獨立猶束柴。

Since my own son met with calamity,
it would be out of keeping if flowers bloomed.
Poor and old, I gather a shattered heart,
through the long night I clasp broken feelings.
Repute died, what more is there to say?—
will died, it did not have to keep in harmony.
Sick old man with no progeny,
I stand alone, like a bundle of kindling.

IX

霜似敗紅芳，剪啄十數雙。
參差呻細風，喲喝沸淺江。
泣凝不可消，恨壯難自降。
空遺就日影，怨彼小書窗。

Frost seems to have ruined red blossoms,
cutting and pecking dozens of pairs.
Here and there groaning in faint breeze,
fish-mouths making bubbles on the shallow
    river.
Tears freeze and cannot melt,
resentment grows vigorous, hard to tame.
In vain there remains the shadow of former
    days,
and I hate that small window of my study.

Much in this poem cycle is so private as to be virtually
unintelligible, but some things are clear. Beginning with an
analogy between the fallen buds and the cloth in which his
child was wrapped, Meng Jiao moves into an analogy between
the buds and his infant that grows increasingly complex.
Ducklings diving under the water and fledgling crows leaving

the nest recall the fall of the apricot buds (falling blossoms were conventionally described as "flying" loose, *fei* 飛). But the ducklings flying up out of the waves and the fledgling crows catching the wind strengthen the singular analogy between the unseasonable destruction of the apricot buds and the death of his own child, neither of which will rise again.

In the third poem of the sequence the singular analogy becomes, through sympathetic resonance, a question of responsibility; and the structure of analogies leads to explicit interpretation: "It must have been that single thread of tears / that entered the heart of this springtime tree." There are peculiar associations of fabric and thread, from the "knife" (or "scissors") of the frost, to the baby's clothing appearing on the ground, and here to the poet's tears of mourning, which become a "thread" that enters the "heart" (heartwood, "trunk") of the tree and results in the death of the apricot buds.

In this cycle we again confront questions of the moral order of Nature and its relation to the human moral order. A purely literary metaphor becomes a deeper analogy, which becomes in turn sympathetic resonance; when priority is established in sympathetic resonance, there is the appearance of causality and moral responsibility. But the process of generating analogies and interpretations does not stop here. In the fourth poem of the cycle Meng Jiao establishes an inverse resonance and shifts the responsibility away from himself. There was an alternation between the waxing and the waning of the moon and the growth and death of his child. The initial impulse is innocent enough, using the phases of the moon to illustrate the brevity of the infant's life. But this quickly becomes reciprocal causality, as the waxing moon steals away the baby's life. In this version the apricot buds need not enter the system; they act on their own responsibility, "willingly" falling to earth.

By the next poem Meng Jiao has come up with yet another interpretation. Not only was he not responsible for the destruction of the apricot buds, he walked with special care so as not to harm the roots of the tree. That solicitous care he showed toward an entity lower in the hierarchy of being was not matched in Heaven's treatment of him. In the remaining poems in the series, the process of association reels out of control: the trunk (*xin* 心, also "heart") of the apricot seems to become a dying tree full of holes, while Meng himself, gathering up a "shattered heart" (broken pieces of wood?), becomes a bundle of kindling. He is both subject and object, cause and victim. Inverting the venerable Confucian principle of "breeding life from life," *shengsheng* 生生, Meng Jiao describes his face as "breeding death from death," *sisi* 死死.

Frozen buds, fallen stars, drops of oil, frozen tears, fish making bubbles on the surface of the water—images succeed one another in dizzying succession, each attached to some fragment of analogical interpretation, none of which goes far enough to make sense. In the end there can be only an angry rejection of the image, the shadow—presumably that of the apricot tree—that he cannot bear to behold.

Without the protective distance of irony, the Mid-Tang drive to explain and find meaning easily becomes the language of madness. The opacity of the world, its resistance to stable interpretation, is sometimes conjoined with the suspicion that any purposeful intelligence at work in it might be malevolent or casually cruel. In this recurrent suspicion the few decades of the Mid-Tang are perhaps unique in the history of Chinese civilization.

In the following poem by Li He, one of the most bizarre pieces of the period, the poet offers an interpretation ostensibly to exonerate the god of intentional malice. Li He evokes the demonic world of the ancient poem "Calling back the Soul" 招魂, populated by monstrous beasts eager to devour the speaker. Among the several interpretations of "Calling back the Soul," one version has it composed to bring back the distraught spirit of Qu Yuan ("he who wears orchids strung from his sash"), wandering in exile.

Figures of eating and being eaten run throughout the poem. "Palm-licking" refers to the legend that bears, hungry from their winter hibernation, sustained themselves by licking their own palms (bears paws were considered a delicacy in ancient cuisine). "Licking their chops" might be the appropriate association in the present context. Bao Jiao was a hermit who refused to eat anything except what he had grown himself; discovering that he had eaten dates that he had not planted, he spat them out and died on the spot. Likewise, Confucius' favorite disciple, Yan Hui, was famous for eating simply and died young.

The final line refers to a contextual explanation for the composition of the "Heaven-Questions" 天問 in the *Chuci*, an explanation offered by the Eastern Han exegete Wang Yi. Qu Yuan supposedly composed the "Heaven-Questions" when he saw wall paintings illustrating Heaven and Earth and gods and spirits. According to Wang Yi the choice of the phrasing "Heaven-Questions" rather than the more natural "Questioning Heaven," *wen Tian* 問天, was because Heaven was too exalted to be questioned.

Li He, *Don't Go out the Gate!*
公無出門 (20831)

天迷迷，地密密。
熊虺食人魂，霜雪斷人骨。
嗾犬狺狺相索索，舐掌偏宜佩蘭客。
帝遣乘軒災自滅，天星點劍黃金軛。
我雖跨馬不得還，歷陽湖波大如山。
毒虯相視振金環，狻猊猭貐吐嚵涎。
鮑焦一世披草眠，顏回廿九鬢毛斑。
顏回非血衰，鮑焦不違天。
天畏遭啣囓，所以致之然。
分明猶懼公不信，公看呵壁書問天。

Heaven beclouds and bewilders,
Earth keeps its secrets close.
Bear-ogres eat men's souls,
snow and frost snap men's bones.

Dogs are unleashed, their mouths loll open,
    sniffing after prey,
those who lick palms find him just right,
    the man who wears orchids strung from his sash.

The god sends a carriage to ride,
    afflictions then vanish,
stars of heaven fleck his sword,
    the carriage-yoke is gold.

Though I set my horse cantering,
    I cannot make it go back,
waves on Lake Liyang
    are large as mountains.
Venomous dragons stare at me,
    shaking metal coils,
griffin and chimera spit
    ravenous drool.

Bao Jiao spent a whole lifetime
    sleeping in the grass;
Yan Hui at twenty-nine
    had locks streaked with white.

It was not that Yan Hui had grown infirm,
nor did Bao Jiao disobey Heaven.
Heaven dreaded lest they be chewed and
    gnawed,
and for that reason made it so.

It's so perfectly clear, but still I fear
    you don't believe—
just look at him yelling at the wall,
    writing out "Questioning Heaven."

The poem opens with echoes of "Calling back the Soul." The soul is lost in darkness: Heaven and Earth are closed off to it. In "Calling back the Soul" the shaman, sent by the High God, warns the soul against journeying to distant regions and tells the soul that if only it returns, it can enjoy all the pleasures of the great house. In Li He the god sends a carriage to offer protection to the good man, surrounded by demonic creatures that seek to eat him, but the speaker cannot get back. At last the poet explains that the god kills good men only to keep them from being chewed up and eaten. What sort of universe is this?

The topography of Li He's poem differs from that of "Calling back the Soul." In "Calling back the Soul" demonic forces lay in all directions, but in the far distance. In contrast, the message in the title of Li He's poem is "don't go out the gate"; hungry demons seem close around. Meng Jiao wrote (19858):

出門即有礙，誰謂天地寬。

When you go out the gate, there's a stumbling-
    block right here—
Who claims Heaven and Earth are broad?

Heaven and Earth are no less closed up in Li He's poem, but here if you go out the door, you meet the "eater-of-souls," the *xionghui*. Everywhere there is the danger of being eaten: dogs are unleashed, and the bears are hungry; the wandering soul of the good man is prey.

The Lord of Heaven intervenes in this world of terror, just as he intervened in "Calling back the Soul." Rescue seems imminent: there is a carriage to bear off the good man and a holy sword, dotted with star patterns, to defend him. What happens then is not clear: the next stanza might be a flashback, but it might also be that the god who promised to save him has deserted him. We see him mounted in the wilderness, unable to make it back to the safety of the gate, left in a world with huge waves, poisonous dragons, "griffin and chimera," the *yayu* and *suanni* monsters, drooling and ready to devour him.

All this requires some explanation, an interpretation, and Li He proposes a hypothesis that, in the context, is a dark sophistry. The Qu Yuan figure of the poem is compared to Bao Jiao and Yan Hui, whom Heaven killed because it was afraid they would be eaten. Yan Hui himself ate simply from his single bamboo plate, and Bao Jiao died from eating only once what he did not produce himself—he perished only when he went out. We think of the hibernating bear that lives by licking the oils of its own palms. They were good; they did not disobey Heaven; yet they were destroyed—so that they would not be *xiannie*, "chewed upon."

That is the explanation; it's so "clear," *fenming* 分明; but you still don't believe. And at the end Li He offers the strangest, most illogical proof of his hypothesis, an image of dissatisfaction, of unanswered and unanswerable questions. He points to a Qu Yuan figure, no longer outside the gate in peril, but facing a wall, yelling questions at it in the disrespectful form of "questioning Heaven." When Meng Jiao planned to "question Heaven about a few things," *wen Tian sansi yu* 問天三四語, he at last came to understand that this was a waste of voice (20026):

一寸地上語，高天何由聞。

Words from this speck of mind on earth—
how could high Heaven hear them?

Li He offers an explanation we are not intended to believe, a parody of authoritative explanation that casts doubt on the moral order of the universe. He uses the form of explanation as an index of the inexplicable, of a Heaven that bewilders and an Earth that keeps its secrets.

Coming here to the limits of interpretation and explanation, we may turn to two poems in a very different key, poems, like Han Yu's and Meng Jiao's, that are concerned with the death of a child. These are Bai Juyi's retrospective poems on his daughter Golden Chimes.

Thinking of Golden Chimes
念金鑾子　(22207–8)

I

衰病四十身，嬌癡三歲女。
非男猶勝無，慰情時一撫。
一朝捨我去，魂影無處所。
況念夭化時，嘔啞初學語。
始知骨肉愛，乃是憂悲聚。
唯思未有前，以理遣傷苦。
忘懷日已久，三度移寒暑。
今日一傷心，因逢舊乳母。

Sick and frail, a body in its forties,
naive and charming, a girl of three years.
Not a boy, but better than none at all,
I cherished her and comforted myself.
One morning she left me and went away,
soul and image were nowhere to be found.
Still more I think of her passing on so young,
prattling and just learning to speak.
Now I know that to dote on flesh and bone
is in fact the assembly of worries and grief.
I thought back on the time before she was born
and used reason to drive out the bitter pain.
She had long been out of my mind,
thrice had seasons of heat and cold passed.
Then today my heart was struck with pain,
because I met her former wet nurse.

II

與爾爲父子，八十有六旬。
忽然又不見，邇來三四春。
形質本非實，氣聚偶成身。
恩愛元是妄，緣合暫爲親。
念茲庶有悟，聊用遣悲辛。
暫將理自奪，不是忘情人。

You and I were father and child
for eight hundred and sixty days.
Then all at once you were unseen again,
and since then it's been three springs or so.
Flesh and form are no solid thing,
qi gathers and makes a body by chance.
Love and doting are delusory at the core,
a chance of fate made you my kin a while.
I think on this hoping to be enlightened,
thereby to drive out pangs of pain.
For a while I use reason to get hold of myself—
I am not a man immune to feeling.

Bai Juyi's rambling and discursive style sought to convey the immediacy of feeling in a way appreciably different from the eighth-century norm. Its apparent artlessness conceals a controlled departure from deep habits of poetic composition.

We might consider the "proper" way to have written the first poem of the pair: it should have followed the order of experience, beginning with the encounter with Golden Chimes's wet nurse and then moving on to reflection on his sense of loss. That would have been the "stirring and response," *ganying* 感應, that was supposed to be the ground of poetry.

Bai Juyi does something quite different in the first poem, framing the very impulse to interpret and holding it up for reflection. He begins with the loss, then moves to a past act of interpretation as consolation, a means to get the pain of loss under control. The interpretive consolation was not a failure; for three years he managed to put the pain out of his mind. But in the closing couplet he meets the wet nurse, and the consolation fails. Bai Juyi does not phrase it that way; he uses the unnecessarily explicit "because," *yin* 因, to join the encounter and the feeling. Although the poem contrasts involuntary emotion and reflective interpretation, that contrast has itself become an act of reflective interpretation.

In the second poem Bai Juyi returns to the attempt to formulate a consolation in the transitoriness of the body and of human affection. Again in the end the consolation fails, in this case not over the long span, but over the short span of formulating the present consolation. The last line tells us that reason, *li* 理, simply does not work. And Bai Juyi's observation about the power of feeling to dominate reason is itself reasonable.

Both the long-span consolation interrupted by the chance encounter and the short-span consolation interrupted because the poet knows better are ways of framing these acts of interpreting his daughter's death as "mere consolation," motivated constructs inadequate to contain the reality of human feeling. This is essentially identical to what Liu Zongyuan did with Han Yu's outrageous theory of Heaven, framing and limiting the interpretive act by the imputation of a circumstantial motive. Though not explicit, the same is true of Meng Jiao's "Apricots Untimely Dead." We read his interpretive acts as the desperate constructs of a man unhinged by grief.

These variations on the act of "mere interpretation" mark the discovery of subjectivity as such. Subjectivity had earlier been more or less successfully integrated with ideology; there was no essential disjunction between inner life and the understanding of "how things are." In Bai Juyi's poems we have the subject touched by feelings for which the understanding of "reason" or "natural principle," *li*, is inadequate (and initiating the opposition between feeling and natural principle that would become so prominent in later centuries). This version of reason including the limits of reason and conceptualizing interpretive acts as motivated creates a space for the "subject" outside his public claims. In the other cases we have discussed, individual interpretation implies a subject who makes the interpretation but who cannot be contained by it. In the medieval phase of received wisdom, the self could be represented and its operations explained. In this new world of the Mid-Tang, subjectivity is located "behind" the explanations it offers and the interpretations it generates. The discovery of stubborn subjectivity is part of what we can call the "private sphere," which we first begin to find in the Mid-Tang.

Crocodiles, blows of fate, and above all, death—in all these cases the act of interpretation is offered against some absolute and threatening external determination. For the culture, however, the most important consequences of acts of individual interpretation will not lie in these, but in situations where far less is at stake. Here interpretation can shape the small world, rather than merely responding to powerful external forces. In the Mid-Tang we see a growing complicity between acts of literary interpretation and private life: building gardens, making miniatures, "home improvement."

❖

Wit and the Private Life

Individual interpretation in the Mid-Tang was by no means
confined to large questions of Heaven, death, and destruction.
Its most characteristic form may have been a playful cleverness, in which little was at stake and the act of interpretation
seemed gratuitous. Such play of wit was often linked to the
small pleasures of domestic life; for example, the gustatory
delight, both seasonal and local, in bamboo shoots.

Bai Juyi, *Eating Bamboo Shoots*
食筍 (22038)

此州乃竹鄉，春筍滿山谷。
山夫折盈抱，抱來早市鬻。
物以多爲賤，雙錢易一束。
置之炊甑中，與飯同時熟。
紫籜坼故錦，素肌擘新玉。
每日遂加餐，經時不思肉。
久爲京洛客，此味常不足。
且食勿踟躕，南風吹爲竹。

This province is truly a land of bamboo,
in spring the sprouts fill valleys and hills.
Men of the hills snap them in armfuls,
and bring them to market as soon as they can.
Things are cheapest when plentiful,
for a pair of coppers a whole bunch can be had.
Just put them into the cooking pot,
and they will be done along with the rice.
Purple sheaths shred their ancient brocade,

> their pale flesh snaps newfound jade.
> So every day I add to my fare,
> through their whole season I yearn not for meat.
> I was long resident in Chang'an and Luoyang,
> and never had my fill of the taste of these.
> Eat while you can, don't hesitate,
> soon south winds will blow them into bamboo.

The noble bamboo, traditional emblem of steadfastness, is here, in its infant form, a taste treat and a commodity. Its abundance makes it a bargain, and it is no less appreciated for that. The joys of acquisition are equal to the joys of eating, although the latter are not to be despised—Bai Juyi even includes a couplet for us on the best way to prepare bamboo shoots.

The difference between the common "high" literary image of bamboo and these tasty shoots is also the difference between the usual sense of the "poetic" and this willfully rambling verse on homey pleasures. The style is supposed to suggest natural innocence and a freshness like that of the speculative vegetable. As if to mark how militantly unpoetic his poem is as a whole, Bai Juyi includes a lurid, mock-poetic couplet, describing an almost erotic stripping of the little vegetable.

> Purple sheaths shred their ancient brocade,
> their pale flesh snaps newfound jade.

This sudden change in register foregrounds the act of representing something "poetically." As the poet strips away the purple sheaths to the white flesh, the humble bamboo shoot is "adorned" with figures (in traditional China, as in Europe, literary figuration was itself figured as clothing). Yet this act of poetic adornment becomes ironic, even comic, when framed by the apparent simplicity of diction in the poem as a whole.

The parody of poetic adornment prepares us for the even more comic couplet that follows, in which Bai Juyi does the same thing to classical allusion that he had just done to poetic diction.

So every day I add to my fare,
through their whole season I yearn not for meat.

This couplet unmistakably recalls *Analects* VII.13, which tells
that when Confucius heard a performance of the ancient
ceremonial Shao music, "for three months [a whole season]
he did not taste meat," *sanyue buzhi rouwei* 三月不知肉味. The
Mid-Tang vegetarian gourmet inserts himself in the place of
the Sage's lingering cultural awe. Such affectionate spoofing
of two forms of authoritative discourse—high poetic diction
and the Confucian classic—marks a changed relation to received culture. Such authoritative modes of discourse make
no absolute claims on the writer, either to accept or reject; he
is free to use them for his own purposes.

"Eating Bamboo Shoots" is characteristic of the Mid-Tang
in lavishing attention on what is small and granting it an excess of value and significance. Bai Juyi takes special care to
remind us how plentiful and "cheap," *jian* 賤 (also "humble,"
"of low degree"), the bamboo shoots are, how the gatherers
bring them to market "as soon as they can" in the hope of
beating the competition, who will soon produce a glut in the
market. The difference between the value poetically assigned
to the thing and the lesser value it is commonly assumed to
have creates a surplus. This surplus is "witty"; that is, it
comes from the poet's own wits rather than from the thing or
situation in its own right. This interpretive surplus belongs to
the poet; it is something he produced and something he de-
ploys for his amusement. To be explicit about the economic
metaphor (which Bai Juyi invites by his frequent attention to
commodity values), the poet takes raw material of little worth
and processes it poetically into a finished product that is
worth more than the raw material; and the surplus of value
added is seen as belonging to the poet. As with so many other
Mid-Tang interests, this is a way of asserting possession, of
marking something as one's own.

The production of something of value from humble material is not limited to the domain of words; sometimes the

physical world must be modified for the sake of interpretation. When the poet also uses his wit to make and arrange things, the act of interpretation becomes indistinguishable from staged domestic pleasures, with the poet's tangible possessions as stage props. Smallness, even miniaturization, is essential to produce the "surplus" of interpretation. Princess Taiping's great park, stretching from the walls of Chang'an to Mount Zhongnan, will not do. Princess Taiping can only contemplate possession. The Mid-Tang poet can appropriate the external possession, swallowing it up within an interpretation that is obviously larger than the thing itself. The thing comes to have value only in and through the interpretation. The act of interpretation becomes the experience of the thing, the significant surplus measured against the thing's small size, modest value, and everydayness. Others just consume the bamboo shoots; Bai Juyi makes them into a durable product.

The older poetics of stirring and response had been sequential; experience came first and the poetic text was the outcome. In the Mid-Tang a new, and often explicit, reciprocity takes shape between poetry and experience. Things are deployed in small domestic spaces for the sake of writing poems, and poems are written for the staged experience of these things. The deployment of things and the arrangement of space are thus also part of the surplus of the poet's wit and thereby his possession.

The discourse of ownership, in the sense of things belonging to the poet alone, again plays a crucial role in this process, with the poet calling attention to exclusionary boundaries. In one way or another such poems often postulate an external observer or point of view, sometimes introduced by the phrase "Don't tell me X." This person sees the object of the poet's attention as merely small, humble, and ordinary. Such a common-sense perspective from an outsider guarantees the singularity of the poet's interpretation, that it "belongs to" the poet alone. Assertion of smallness or triviality of the object or assemblage is essential, ensuring that all value lies in the surplus of interpretation.

This was a moment of great importance in China's elite culture. It marked the transition from the great medieval theme of reclusion, which defined the private purely in negative terms as the rejection of the public, to the creation of a "private sphere," embodied in a private space that was at once within the public world while at the same time enclosed and protected from it.[1] Private space is possessed, and possession is achieved through the surplus of interpretation. Han Yu and Bai Juyi construct miniature pools. There is no absolute right of property: the emperor can confiscate the land and the little bodies of water whenever he pleases, but he cannot appropriate what Han Yu and Bai Juyi have made of those miniature pools. The small garden comes to replace the wild mountain landscape as the locus of freedom, and the meaning of freedom changes accordingly.

The earlier world of the recluse was not owned space, nor was it bounded space. To choose such a world was always a potentially public statement, a criticism of the government in power. It shared in that older Chinese conceptualization of space in terms of centers rather than boundaries. When the medieval official decided to give up his post and become a recluse, there was no clear frontier between the two worlds, only a "here" and a "there." In Kong Zhigui's 孔稚珪 (447–501) "North Mountain Proclamation" 北山移文, a hermit decided to leave his mountain in answer to a call to court, and wild Nature denounced his treason with anthropomorphic demonstrations of indignation. The departure is clearly not the physical act of leaving itself but the intention and direction. In contrast, the construction of boundaries is of prime importance in the creation of private space. Such space is often miniature; it is the large within the small, ambiguously a microcosmic reflection of the larger world and the poet's surplus of interpretation. Such private space is usually artifactual,

---

[1] Using the term "private sphere" risks calling to mind Habermas and the debates on the existence of a "public sphere" in China. As will become clear, the issue that I am addressing here is quite distinct.

both in the physical sense of being constructed and in the conceptual sense of being constituted through interpretation. Princess Taiping could never truly own Nature on her vast estate; her claim to possession was a mere display of political power, which fluctuated with the unstable currents of court politics and eventually destroyed her. On the smaller, Mid-Tang scale, Nature can be owned. The problem is that it is no longer purely natural; Nature provides the raw materials that are constructed and interpreted by the poet.

By "private sphere" I mean a cluster of objects, experiences, and activities that belong to a subject apart from the social whole, whether state or family. In the creation of private space, some assertion of superfluity and play is essential. Anything that is serious or "matters" has, by definition, entered China's fractal cosmology and been subsumed into the larger interests of the state and the moral order of society. As the *Great Learning* 大學 tells us, self-examination and self-cultivation lead inexorably upward to the family, the state, and the world. Such a devouring structure of totalization begs for a reservation, some arena of activity and experience that is not entirely swallowed up by the imperatives of the social and political whole.[2] But that abstract "sphere" requires a space—an ambiguous space like the stage—where something can happen inside the emperor's land that is, at the same time, not part of the emperor's land. This space was, above all, the garden, and although there had long been parks and gardens in China, they did not mean what the garden came to mean in later imperial civilization.

The private sphere was a fragile construct. It could exist only by constantly asserting its own superfluity, which made

[2] The constitution of the private sphere simultaneously produced a sharper awareness of how the small particulars of life are implicated in large social issues. Bai Juyi was the poet of domestic pleasures par excellence, but he was also the poet who expressed shame that the rice he ate came from the labors of farmers. The fully conscious relation of the individual to the social whole is possible only when one has developed a sense of the individual apart from the social whole.

ownership possible. The space in which the private sphere appeared was very much contested territory (since any structure of totalizing power, by its very nature, resists a reservation). The emperor could always confiscate the garden and execute its maker, but such draconian measures did not enable him to lay claim to the surplus. The literati themselves, deeply ambivalent, waged the real contest for private space on behalf of the state and emperor. Essayists would often look at the pavilion or garden of an official and claim to infer from its construction the quality of his governance. Private space was always a space of reflection, reproducing in miniature the image of one thing or another. Dramatically positioned rocks recalled famous mountains, and small pools contained the diminutive image of the heavens. It is precisely in this contest between a claim of superfluous play and serious reflection of the larger world that these private spaces most closely resemble the stage or the motion picture screen, within whose bounded spaces that ancient struggle is still waged.

Many Mid-Tang concerns can be traced to the work of Du Fu, and the private sphere first gains prominence in his work. Du Fu assumed the role of the self-consciously public poet, in ways that his contemporaries, who were often far more deeply engaged in public events, did not. The possibility of representing a distinct realm of private life goes hand in hand with the representation of political engagement as something to be affirmed, rather than accepted as a given. Du Fu demarcated and celebrated domestic space; he used poetry reciprocally with domestic action, and he offered the characteristically "superfluous" interpretation. Porches had surely been repaired, overabundant patches of bamboo cut back, and trellises removed long before poetry was written on these topics. When and how such things became the subject matter for poetry are topics of interest. Du Fu's poetry does not yet bring us to the Mid-Tang world of staged miniatures, but we do begin to see the appropriation of domestic activity for poetry and the role of superfluous interpretation in that process.

Although Du Fu's interest in domestic space can be found earlier, it is clearest in the poetry he wrote in Chengdu. Public and private, large and small, are thrown into sharpest relief when the political world breaks in upon private space and threatens to destroy it, as happened to Du Fu repeatedly. After being forced to flee a mutiny by the Chengdu garrison, in 764 Du Fu returned to his cottage on the outskirts of the city. It was at this time that he wrote "Broken Boat" 破船 (10747), a play of interpretation around the object of its title, the boat that had been, before its ruin, both the speculative means of sailing downriver and the means by which he speculated on sailing downriver as he drifted in it near his famous "thatched cottage" writing poetry. Finding his boat sunk and ruined on his return, Du Fu lamented the loss and concluded:[3]

> 所悲數奔竄，白屋難久留。
>
> What grieves me is frequent hiding and flight,
> that in a plain cottage I cannot linger long.

The experience and the process of poetic reflection teach Du Fu the desire for a private space protected from the public world, where the stage props of his fantasy are not destroyed. Instead of far travels, the poet wants to be able to stay put and dream of far travels.

In "Deck by the Water" 水檻 (10746), from the same year, Du Fu takes stock of a part of his dwelling that had fallen into disrepair during his absence. Here poetic interpretation interposes itself in the simple task of making repairs and turns those repairs into something no longer entirely simple. Du Fu makes a poetic move that would become commonplace in the Mid-Tang, imposing an overlarge interpretation on something small, thereby calling attention to the interpretive act. In contrast to the Mid-Tang poet, however, Du Fu is not comfortable with such an obviously "unnatural" interpreta-

---

[3] For a full discussion of this poem, see Stephen Owen, *Traditional Chinese Poetry and Poetics: An Omen of the World* (Madison: University of Wisconsin Press, 1985), pp. 116–21.

tion and attempts to redeem the situation with a more natural one.

蒼江多風飆，雲雨晝夜飛。
茅軒駕巨浪，焉得不低垂。
遊子久在外，門戶無人持。
高岸尚爲谷，何傷浮柱攲。
扶顚有勸誡，恐貽識者嗤。
既殊大廈傾，可以一木支。
臨川視萬里，何必欄檻爲。
人生感故物，慷慨有餘悲。

Winds often gust hard on the gray river,
rain flies from clouds both day and night.
This thatched porch mounted on mighty
    waves—
how could it help sagging down low?
Its owner has long traveled abroad,
and there was none to maintain the
    place.
If even high slopes turn to valleys,
why care that its posts are leaning?
A precept tells us: "Support what totters"—
I suspect I'll be laughed at by those who
    know it.
Yet this differs from a mighty hall's
    collapse—
it can be propped up with a single beam.
You can see thousands of miles from the river's
    side,
so what need is there for a porch?
But people are moved by familiar things,
and I am overwhelmed by grief.

Whether to repair a sagging deck had never been a question that was felt to merit serious poetic treatment; when Du
Fu takes up the question, however, the poem becomes self-
reflexive, turning back to his own interest in the topic. The
poem implicitly seeks to answer why this matters to him and
why the serious genre of poetry should concern itself with
something so trivial and commonplace. This opposition be-

tween "high" and "low" is mirrored in the transformation of the deck itself, formerly standing straight and secure, offering a river vista appropriate for poetry, and now sagging toward collapse. This opposition is stylistically imitated in the second couplet, moving from high poetic diction ("mounted on mighty waves") to more ordinary language.

Discovering that his deck is on the point of collapse, Du Fu begins to argue with himself: "if even high slopes turn to valleys," if dynasties fall and the very earth changes, why should I care about so unimportant a thing as my deck? Du Fu answers his question by poetically inflating the significance of the deck with an outrageous application of a passage in the *Analects* (XVI.6), in which Confucius enjoins us to "support what / whoever totters," *fudian* 扶顛. Confucius' precept admits a wide latitude of interpretation, but it was clearly not intended to apply to porches.

Du Fu's attempt to universalize the phrase in this way, making the minor thing yet another case of the larger principle, instead calls attention to the *difference* between the serious principle and the triviality of the present circumstance. It becomes comic, in the same way that Bai Juyi's evocation of Confucius' response to the Shao music was comic when applied to eating bamboo shoots. Bai Juyi, however, clearly intended a comic effect in his echo of the *Analects*; it is unlikely that Du Fu did. Du Fu cannot help, however, being aware of the comic incongruity, and in the line that follows, he anticipates educated mockery of his interpretive excess (an excess of the form "applying a phrase out of context," *duanzhang quyi* 斷章取義). The poem includes a mocking or disbelieving external perspective to confirm the surplus or excess of the poet's interpretive act.

The poem next tries to shore up his collapsing allusion to the *Analects* by recalling the conventional architectural metaphor of the state as a "mighty hall." He cannot salvage the figural edifice of state, but propping up the empirical deck does lie within his limited powers. Yet no matter how much Du Fu strains to allegorize his domestic structure, it remains stubbornly no more than a deck, ironizing his attempts at interpretation and foregrounding their excess.[4] Du Fu is seeking to answer the question why he cares about fixing the deck. The citation of the ancient precept fails and wins mockery. He reminds himself that the deck is not even necessary, that the vista downriver can be seen just as well without it.

In the final couplet Du Fu attempts to naturalize his concern, to find a poetically acceptable motive that explains his interpretive excess (just as Liu Zongyuan naturalized Han Yu's excessive interpretation of Heaven by suggesting that something must have upset him). Du Fu's final explanation is at least partially credible: he appeals to a general resistance to decay and loss that does indeed unite the large and the small cases. It is credible precisely because it is a personal motive. The closing statement of grief authenticates the discovery of the correct explanation: the poem need pose no further hypotheses. Having identified the true source of his concern, all that remains is to respond to it. We are bothered when any "familiar thing," *guwu* 故物, goes to ruin; it is our natural impulse to prevent it, to take arms against decay even if it is only with a single beam.

The commonplace ideological core of the poem is that the small thing is the microcosm of the large: if you want to rectify the empire, you begin with yourself or your family. The poem, however, breaks apart cosmology; it calls attention to the disparity between the large and the small. The "close at hand" application of the *Analects* becomes a mockery of that principle, which even the naturalizing interpretation at the end cannot entirely heal. Du Fu has circumscribed a small world of concern that cannot effectively be explained and

---

[4] Some measure of the changes occurring in Du Fu's work can be seen in the comparison of this poem to "Taking down a Trellis" 除架 (11072) from Du Fu's stay in Qinzhou just five years earlier. There Du Fu tags a broken-down vegetable trellis with a well-known phrase from the *Shijing* describing the fate of dynasties. There is a tension between large and small, grand and trivial, but no irony has taken shape in that tension: Du Fu does not yet imagine anyone laughing at the application.

justified as a microcosm of the large world. In effect, this is private space; it cannot be persuasively integrated with the totality of state and universe. The small thing as the microcosm of the large was the medieval assumption, and a change on one scale had echoes in the other. This mirroring of the large in the small survives in Du Fu and the Mid-Tang writers as a poetic trope, but often as the ironic ground on which one calls attention to the *difference* between the large and the small. This means, in effect, that the small can no longer be subsumed by the large, that it is not "serious" and thus can be a private domain to be possessed.

Du Fu's evocation of the mocking scholars who will scoff at his application of the *Analects* phrase finds its most common Mid-Tang transformation in the poet's address to an invisible interlocutor, "Don't tell me X." The reader recognizes immediately that the prohibited observation is the commonsense judgment. This commonsense perspective creates an ironized "private perspective," and the Mid-Tang poet, unlike Du Fu, declares his preference for the private perspective. This private, domestic space, the garden as Nature possessed, is the site of imaginative play revealed as such.

In Bai Juyi's "A Small Pond Newly Dug on the Premises of the Public Office Building" 官舍內新鑿小池 (22021), we have the artifactual miniature of nature, a literal "reflection" of Heaven, for whose significance and value the poet must argue.

> 簾下開小池，盈盈水方積。
> 中底鋪白沙，四隅甃青石。
> 勿言不深廣，但取幽人適。
> 泛灩微雨朝，泓澄明月夕。
> 豈無大江水，波浪連天白。
> 未如床席前，方丈深盈尺。
> 清淺可狎弄，昏煩聊漱滌。
> 最愛曉暝時，一片秋天碧。

Beneath the drapes appeared a small pond,
welling now with waters massed.

In the middle its bottom is spread with white
    sand,
its four corners tiled with green stone.
Don't tell me it is not deep or broad!—
it just suits the whims of a private man.
It rolls with ripples on dawns of light rain,
it is clear and deep on bright moonlit eves.
Of course, there are the Great River's waters
whose waves are white touching horizons;
but better what lies before your own couch,
a square yard, a full foot deep.
Clear and shallow, I can treat it with playful
    familiarity;
when confused and troubled, I can wash myself
    there.
But I love most of all the dark before dawn
a single sheet of green of autumn's skies.

Anyone who reads this poem after wide reading in Mid-Tang poetry and particularly in the poetry of Bai Juyi will probably have a sense of having read it before. The poem shares a number of core elements with many other poems: the pool is a construct that suits the poet's nature and has been made to entertain the poet's private life; it is described in excessive poetic terms; proposed criticisms, revealing a common perspective, are rejected; the poet explicitly declares his love of and preference for the private construct; it offers the illusion of large nature in miniature.

The poem opens by orienting the pond and revealing its scale, followed by a line poetically describing what would seem a much larger body of water: "welling now with waters massed." The pool's virtues are its proximity, its comfortable scale, and, within its small scope, a variety that suits the poet's changing whims. The pool is not only his physical construction; its pleasures are his imaginative construction, whose very playfulness reveals that its attractions are in Bai Juyi's mind rather than generally observable in the pool itself. Particularly significant is *xia'nong* 狎弄, loosely translated as "treat it with playful familiarity." This is an erotic dallying, a delight in an object that need not be treated with reserve and respect. It is a body of water that is owned, as a concubine might be owned; it exists for one's amusement. The small thing that is possessed is explicitly articulated against the large world, the "Great River's waters," and the small thing is preferred.[5] The relation between the large world and the small world and the turn away from the large world to the artifactual miniature is perfectly embodied in the final line, in which the poet chooses to observe the beauty of the predawn skies by looking into the miniature reflection rather than by looking upward.

Constructed nature is safe, protected space, space over which the subject has power and in which he can stage experience. These acts of play are usually self-reflexive interpretations that come back to celebrating the constructed miniature of nature as such. Miniature ponds seem to have been something of a fashion in the early ninth century, for we have also a well-known series of quatrains on the same topic by Han Yu.

Han Yu, *Pond in a Basin*
盆池 (18034–38)

I
老翁眞箇似童兒，汲水埋盆作小池。
一夜青蛙鳴到曉，恰如方口釣魚時。

I mean it, this old man
    is acting just like a kid,
he buried a basin and drew some water
    to make a little pond.
All night long green frogs
    go singing until dawn,
and it's just like when I go
    fishing at Fangkou.

---

[5] Several of the phrases used in this poem recall the tenth of the "Nineteen Old Poems," in which the Weaver Woman stares across the Milky Way.

II

莫道盆池作不成，藕梢初種已齊生。
從今有雨君須記，來聽蕭蕭打葉聲。

Don't tell me my pond in a basin
    is not completely done,
I began planting slips of lotus root
    and now they are growing evenly.
From now on whenever there's rain,
    you have to notice—
come listen to the whistling wind
    and the sound as it beats on the leaves.

III

瓦沼晨朝水自清，小蟲無數不知名。
忽然分散無蹤影，惟有魚兒作隊行。

An earthenware pond at the break of dawn,
    the water naturally clear,
little insects in countless numbers
    whose names I do not know.
All of a sudden they scatter
    leaving no shadow or trace,
and there are only the little fish
    moving in their schools.

IV

泥盆淺小詎成池，夜半青蛙聖得知。
一聽暗來將伴侶，不煩鳴喚鬥雄雌。

How can a basin, shallow and small
    and muddy, make a pond?—
at midnight the green frogs
    by sage instinct understand.
Just listen to how they come in the dark,
    bringing along their companions,
they do not stint on croaks or puffs
    to test which is the stronger.

V

池光天影共青青，拍岸纔添水數瓶。
且待夜深明月去，試看涵泳幾多星。

Light in the pond and rays from the sky
    are both so very green,

waves dash on shore, and I've added only
  a few pitchers of water.
Just wait until deep in the night
  when the bright moon is gone,
take a look then at how many bright stars
  lie there submerged.

From the opening line of the first poem, we are introduced to a small drama of innocence and staged pleasures. Han Yu is the old man acting like a child, who knows that he is acting like a child, as a true child does not. He stresses the resemblance in the colloquial *zhen'ge* 眞箇, "really," "I mean it," and the stress reminds us that the simple similitude is, in fact, not the case. The distance between the sophisticated old man and the play of naiveté is the same distance between the diminutive reality of the "pond in a basin" and its puffed-up interpretations. Like Bai Juyi, Han Yu creates a stage for an illusion that he knows to be an illusion, and in a common move in the poetry of sensuous illusion, he withdraws into the primarily auditory realm of darkness, to the frogs singing all night long.

The other quatrains contain many of the same moves that we find in Bai Juyi's poems: the rejection of the commonsense observation ("Don't tell me X"), the conscious restriction of attention to the miniature where relative contrasts of scale imitate the relative scale of the large world, and the concluding figure of reflection, in which the large world is literally mirrored in the small. In drawing the frogs by "sage instinct," the artifact becomes Nature; it is the site of a singing contest, described as poetry competitions were described in the same period.

Home and garden are an enclosed space that can be controlled, and their enclosure is a cultural analogy to the frame of a mirror or a work of art, a boundary that the outer world can cross only as reflection or representation. The distance required by a notion of the "aesthetic" usually necessitates such a clear boundary. Arts everywhere reproduce the concerns of the large world within a privileged realm where they can be confronted without threat. Such artifactual spaces belong to their maker and can be displayed as private possession. The problem of display has been resolved in Western civilization by resorting to the pedestal, the frame, or margin of the stage; works of art can "hang" inside the larger world, can rest on pedestals in the large world, or can be performed in the large world, without ever being fully part of it. From the early ninth century on, China developed traditions of staging aesthetic experience in enclosed domestic space. The lures and struggles of the larger world were reproduced in miniature and brought into a complex culture of aesthetic activities, in which poetry came to play the role of commentary, the necessary interpretation that gives the activity value and significance.

Even more clearly than Bai Juyi in his pool poem, Han Yu not only enjoys the pond, he enjoys seeing himself enjoying the pond. Staged pleasures seem to require envisaging oneself in action, seen from the outside. The poet secretly stands among those he addresses: "Don't tell me!" He points to himself and remarks that the figure by the pond is acting like a child. Such theatrical self-consciousness is an essential part of constructing private space; this artifactual and miniature Nature depends upon the poet envisioning himself center stage, interpreting it and enjoying it. This immediately creates a disjunction between the speaker, who always knows better, and the self that is represented. Like the garden itself, the represented self is also a construct, and just as the poet claims that the garden is the microcosm of Nature, he may also claim that the represented self is the very embodiment of the natural man.

For all its apparent simplicity, Bai Juyi's "Newly Planted Bamboo" 新栽竹 (22134) is the perfect paradigm of the garden constructed and interpreted, as well as of the represented self who inhabits it.

> 佐邑意不適，閉門秋草生。
> 何以娛野性，種竹百餘莖。
> 見此階上色，憶得山中情。

有時公事暇，盡日繞欄行。
勿言根未固，勿言陰未成。
已覺庭宇內，稍稍有餘清。
最愛近窗臥，秋風枝有聲。

Having charge of a town suited me not;
I shut my gates as plants of autumn grew.
How could I please my wilderness nature?—
I planted over a hundred stalks of bamboo.
When I see their color over the stairs,
I think back on my mood in the mountains.
At times when I'm free of public work,
I spend all day long walking around the railing.
Don't tell me their roots are not firmly set!
don't tell me their shade is not yet formed!
Already I feel that in house and yard
bit by bit it's abundantly cool and clear.
I love most lying close to the window—
in the autumn wind are its branches' sounds.

The poet begins in dissatisfaction with public responsibility and responds not by going away to the wilderness but by retreating indoors, shutting the gates, and creating a barrier between space inside and space outside. Strangely, within this domestic enclosure he seeks to please his "wilderness nature," *yexing* 野性. In the medieval world of the recluse, the political center was the "inner," *nei* 內, and the wilderness was quintessentially "outer," *wai* 外. Here, however, an inversion has occurred: the garden is the "inner" term, and the domain of public responsibility the "outer." Nevertheless, inner garden space assumes the old role of the wilderness in delighting that aspect of his nature that longs for the wild. The phrasing is particularly significant: the bamboo make him "think back on my mood in the mountains." The bamboo grove is the constructed stimulus, offering a mediated and retrospective experience of wild Nature, an experience that strives impossibly to become immediate. The bamboo grove is a construction of his desire and the site of an illusion that the poet acknowledges as such.

Just as the bamboo grove is surrounded by public space, his experience of the garden is a circular motion around the railing, a day spent walking, as he might have in a linear journey through bamboo groves in the mountains. Like the reflected microcosm, circular motion, so important in garden poetry, is the unlimited within limitation. The experience is, moreover, a bounded span circumscribed by public time. It is a place to be known during "time off" from his public duties.

At this point Bai Juyi introduces the commonsense perspective by forbidding it. It should be noted that apart from the very few who actually visited Bai Juyi's bamboo grove, none of us would have known that his bamboo had not yet taken firm root and were not yet fully grown if Bai Juyi himself had not told us so. This ordinary perspective lets us measure Bai Juyi's surplus of interpretation and overvaluing. Inferring the actual state of the bamboo from Bai Juyi's prohibition, we recognize that Bai's sense of increasing clarity and cool is also illusion.

Then, in the final couplet, the poet does something remarkable. He withdraws further within (apparently no longer fully satisfied by walking around the porch). Here he listens to the sound made by the bamboo. Withdrawing from the domain of sight, where he must confront the discrepancy between the evidence of the senses and the bamboo grove he wishes to have, he enters the realm of hearing, where the illusion of a wild bamboo grove in the mountains can be sustained by the immediate evidence of the senses. But this too is an illusion that he knows to be merely an illusion.

Desire, construction, the staging of pleasure in an enclosed space, the reproduction of the natural as an illusion within the artifactual—all these activities of the private sphere are centered around the poet, not as a social being or as a sensibility, but as a mind with devices adequate to his desires. The poet stages Nature and himself takes center stage as the natural man.

This version of the "private," with its constant attention to being observed from the outside, is ultimately a form of social display, depending on the amused approval of others who are playfully excluded. The possibility of a private sphere is itself a social phenomenon, and these texts reinforce values that are shared by a group, if not by society as a whole. The poems of the miniature garden, like Liu Zongyuan's prose accounts of land purchase in the wilderness, are intended for public circulation, displaying the ingenious mind far more than the secluded terrain.

As a reflecting space that potentially transforms what lies outside, we might consider the way in which private space potentially can subsume social obligations and refigure them. Tang poets were generally reticent about their families. The general rareness of comment makes it seem all the more remarkable when it occurs, as it sometimes does in the poetry of Du Fu and Bai Juyi. With its alliances, prospects, worries, and obligations, the real family bound a person very directly to the large, public world. Social relations within the private sphere would have to be something else, constructing the idea of relations to others just as the garden constructs Nature.

Bai Juyi, *Choosing a Dwelling Place*
in Luoyang 洛下卜居 (22117)

三年典郡歸，所得非金帛。
天竺石兩片，華亭鶴一隻。
飲啄供稻粱，苞裹用茵蓆。
誠知是勞費，其奈心愛惜。
遠從餘杭郭，同到洛陽陌。
下擔拂雲根，開籠展霜翮。
貞姿不可雜，高性宜其適。
遂就無塵坊，仍求有水宅。
東南得幽境，樹老寒泉碧。
池畔多竹陰，門前少人跡。
未請中庶祿，且脫雙驂易。
豈獨爲身謀，安吾鶴與石。

Back from three years in charge of a province,
what I got was not silk and not gold:

Two rocks from India Mountain there,
and a single crane from Huating:
The one I feed with rice and grain;
the others I wrap in fine mats.
I know quite well it's expense and trouble,
I can't help that I care for them.
I brought them from Hangzhou's outskirts afar,
we arrived together in Luoyang's streets.
The burden set down, I brushed roots-of-cloud;
I opened the cage, it spread frosty wings.
Things pure of feature may not mix with others,
high natures deserve what suits them.
So I went to a ward that was free of dust
and sought lodgings that had some waters.
To the southeast I found a quiet place,
its trees were aged, its cold spring green.
Beside a pool, much shade from bamboo,
few tracks of men in front of the gates.
I don't ask the pay of a palace cadet,
I traded away my two-horse team.
I'm not watching out for myself alone—
my rocks and crane must have a haven.

Perhaps Bai Juyi's possession of the rocks and crane resemble the acquisition of a concubine more closely than a marriage ("getting," *de* 得, in the second line, was the proper verb for the acquisition of a concubine but not for finding a wife). In this case the surplus value is displayed not in the amusement afforded to the poet but in the care he lavishes on his favorites. The requisite double perspective is made quite explicit in this poem:

I know quite well it's expense and trouble,
I can't help that I care for them.

The poet admits "knowing better," being able to see things from a conventional perspective; he also makes the essential claim to be the natural man, in being absorbed, unable to help himself. Yet the voice speaking through the poem represents neither of those perspectives: it is a voice of sheer delight in inventing representations of his own excess.

The conclusion, protesting that he acts not on his own behalf but on behalf of his rocks and crane, is clearly tongue-in-cheek, but the form of such a representation of his motives deserves some reflection. As in a standard formula in memorials or poetically in Du Fu's "My Thatched Roof Is Whirled Away by the Autumn Wind," disclaiming personal advantage is essential to authority in public discourse. It is the trope of subordinating the self to "larger" interests. Here the trope survives as a playful form, inverted so that he subordinates himself to the interests of the private sphere, while making the public post of palace cadet represent selfish interests. The structure of relations within the garden is, like the tiny pool, a mirror of those outside, with the difference being that the garden hierarchy is his own creation.

The power of interpretive wit was not confined to the space of the garden. Wit is portable and can turn other places into imitations of the private, constructed space of the garden. Here it is important to keep in mind that this poetry of the private sphere is public; it is given to friends and circulated. The object of display is not the garden but the poet. One of Bai Juyi's most famous poems is set in the mountains, but we recognize immediately that these are not the same mountains where the great medieval recluses lived: not only are they mountains visited in moments of leisure from public responsibility, but an amazed audience quickly gathers to construct a limited space in which the poet stands at the center of attention. In that centering direction of the gaze, the mountains become the garden.

Reciting Poems Alone in the Mountains
山中獨吟 (22069)

人各有一癖，我癖在章句。
萬緣皆以銷，此病獨未去。
每逢美風景，或對好親故。
高聲詠一篇，恍若與神遇。
自爲江上客，半在山中居。
有時新詩成，獨上東巖路。
身倚白石崖，手攀青桂樹。

狂吟驚林壑，猿鳥皆窺覷。
恐爲時所嗤，故就無人處。

Each person has some one addiction,
my addiction is to writing:
All worldly attachments have melted away,
I am left with this sole affliction.
Whenever I chance on a lovely scene,
or face some dear friend or family,
I sing out a poem in a loud voice,
in a daze as if touched by some god.
Since I sojourned here by the River,
I spend half my time in the hills.
There are times when a new poem is finished,
and I go up alone the east cliff road,
I lean against scarps of white stone,
with my hand I pull the green cassia.
Mad chanting alarms the wooded ravines,
birds and gibbons turn all eyes on me.
I'm afraid I'll be mocked by the times,
so I come to this place where no man is.

Bai Juyi is not simply the poet who writes but the poet
who envisions himself writing. Like the garden, behavior is
the consequence of a projective act of imagining "how it will
be." Just as the garden is both artifact and Nature, so the
poet is both self-invented and the natural man, under the
compulsion of an "addiction," *pi* 癖, his love of poetry an
"affliction" or "disease," *bing* 病. That may be true in several
senses. One is the spontaneous bursting into song: "in a daze
as if touched by some god." Another is the poetic wit, which
constructs, which stages experience, and which can never
again unify the poet speaking and the poet represented.

Bai Juyi needed others to mock the empirical garden
whose value he poetically inflated, and here he needs the
conventional perspective of others to speculatively mock his
poems. In fear of their mockery he goes "to this place where
no man is." But even though these are the mountains rather
than the garden, we note at once that this mountain space is
defined by exclusion. Here in theatrical privacy he performs

the poems he has completed beforehand. And although he pretends to exclude his mocking contemporaries, performance speculatively projects his being observed and heard with amazement; he imagines himself as the center of a circle of attention, a fictive audience of birds and gibbons—as well as, of course, of us who read the poem.

There is a small point in this poem that we scarcely notice. Although Bai Juyi speaks of poetic composition as spontaneously bursting into song, he has actually divided the event of poetry into distinct phases of composition and performance. Bai Juyi took special pride in the clumsiness of his poetry, tacitly claiming for it a stylistic naturalness like the naturalness of the naive poet in his miniature garden. But just as large questions of self-conscious artifice hang about the poet and his garden, it is unclear whether the poem is the pure expression of the moment's impulse or something composed with its future performance in mind. It may not be the spontaneous moment itself but the performance and representation of the spontaneous moment.

❖

Ideas of Poetry and Writing
in the Early Ninth Century

The oldest and most authoritative versions of compositional poetics in the Chinese tradition share an insistence on the organic nature of poetic production. Whether social mores, cosmic process, private feeling, or some combination of the three is identified as the motive force behind the text, articulation is seen as originating in some version of Nature rather than purposeful art. The pleasure in literary craft found occasionally in the Han Dynasty provoked a strongly negative reaction: it was, in Yang Xiong's 揚雄 (53 B.C.–A.D. 18) words, "insect carving," *diaochong* 雕蟲, a waste of attention that suggested a susceptibility to moral laxity. Poetic craft became an intense interest during the Southern Dynasties, but theorists continued to take it as a sign of the decay of social mores. In the *Wenxin diaolong* 文心雕龍, the great treatise on literature of the period, Liu Xie 劉協 (ca. 465–ca. 520) did his best to reconcile craft with organic theories of composition, but more often than not the two principles were left in an uneasy conjunction. The seventh century and the first half of the eighth century saw the full development of technical poetics, promising to teach the craft to aspiring versifiers (considering the social demand for reasonably competent composition, such a development is hardly surprising). Denunciations of craft in contemporary poetry diminished but did not disappear. Nevertheless, when attention shifted from the details of the compositional process to larger claims about the nature of poetry, organic theories of composition still held sway.

In the Mid-Tang a relatively new notion of composition became prominent, bridging the opposition between Nature and craft.[1] The couplet or line came to be treated as a *trouvaille*, a lucky find that was first "gotten," *de* 得, then worked into a poem by reflective craft. This newly prominent notion had profound implications for understanding the relation between experience and composition. We begin to see writers acknowledging a temporal disjunction between the putative experience that occasioned the poem and the act of composition, as well as the idea of "working on" a poem. This points toward the idea of poetry as an art rather than a transparent adjunct to experience.

The growing interest in the poetic *trouvaille* was related to the formation of a "transmimetic" aesthetic ("beyond scene," *jingwai* 景外; "beyond image," *xiangwai* 象外; "beyond words," *yanwai* 言外) in the late eighth and early ninth centuries. Here the poetic envisagement was distinguished from empirical sensory experience and from the ability of words to directly represent such experience. As *trouvailles* that are "gotten," such poetic scenes are possessions and signal the poet's singularity of vision.

The intention to write something singular and identifiably belonging to the author was also shared by those who subscribed to a purely organic theory of composition. We may begin by contrasting two very famous and very different accounts of composition in the early ninth century. The first is the central passage from Han Yu's "Letter in Reply to Li Yi" 答李翊書. After describing the long process of study by which he sought to internalize the aims of the ancients and eliminate "worn-out words," *chenyan* 陳言, Han Yu continues:

[1] The interests that I describe in this essay are only one strand in a complex web of various interests in literary composition and literary theory in the eighth century. Perhaps the most striking alternative is the idea of the poet as a true creator, one who competes with the cosmic Fashioner. See Shang Wei, "The Prisoner and the Creator: The Self-Image of the Poet in Han Yü and Meng Chiao," *CLEAR* 16 (Dec. 1994): 19–40.

當其取於心而注於手也，汩汩然來矣。其觀於人也，笑之則以爲
喜譽之則以爲憂，以其猶有人之說者存也。如是者亦有年。然後
浩乎其沛然矣。吾又懼其雜也，迎而距之，平心而察之，其皆醇
也。然後肆焉。雖然，不可以不養也。行之乎仁義之塗，游之乎
詩書之源，無絕其源。終吾身而已矣。氣水也，言浮物也。水大
而物之浮者大小畢浮。氣之與言猶是也，氣勝則言之短長與聲之
高下者皆宜。

When it was seized in the mind and poured out through the
hand, it came in a torrent. Yet when others read it, I considered it a cause for delight if they made fun of it and a cause
for anxiety if they commended me, taking that as a sign that
others' theories still remained.[2] It was like this for some
years more, and only then did it become a streaming flood.
But then again I feared lest it be impure; when I stood back
from it and faced it, examining it with an unprejudiced
mind, I found that it was entirely pure. Only then did I give
myself free rein. Nevertheless one may not fail to nurture it,
making it go along the path of Fellow-Feeling and Right,
making it roam in the sources of the Poems and Documents,
never letting it stray from its course and never cutting it off
from its source—and that is how it is to be for the rest of my
life.

Breath [*qi*] is water; words are floating things. When the
waters are great, all things, whether large or small, float
upon it. The relation between breath and words is like this.
When the breath is full, the length of periods in the words
and the level of the sound is always appropriate.[3]

This is a variation on the standard account of "study,"
xue 學, in which proper models and critical reflection are in-
ternalized until they become "second nature." This leads to
spontaneous production (or the reproduction of norms). Han
Yu's most characteristic imprint on this part of the theory is
his anxiety about contamination. The threatening impurities
are, not elements defined as morally wrong, but elements

[2] It is possible to interpret the 說 here as *yue*, to "fancy" or "please,"
for "a sign that what pleased others still remained."

[3] Ma Qichang, ed., *Han Changli wenji jiaozhu* (Shanghai: Zhonghua
shuju, 1964), p. 99.

belonging to others and winning their favor. The empirical proof of the morally pure text is found in the universal contempt of others. Even if we read this as a defensive move, it remains a defensive move with radical implications. The governing antithesis of the passage is the "pure," *chun* 醇, and the "impure" or "mixed," *za* 雜, defined by the presence of "others' theories." This is the discovery of unique identity by the exclusion of the foreign: like China purged of Buddhism, envisioned in Han's "Memorial on the Buddha's Bone," or Princess Taiping's park south of Changan, the text must "belong to no one else." The final goal, the spontaneous realization of purified identity, is the literary transformation of Mencius' "flooding *qi*," *haoran zhi qi* 浩然之氣 (*qi* is here both "energy" and "breath") that carries a freight of words whose organization follows the medium of *qi*. Its rhythms are supposed to be natural and irregular, thus irreproducible, in contrast to the formal parallel rhetoric that is shared and reproducible.

The second passage is the famous anecdote from Li Shangyin's "A Short Biography of Li He" 李賀小傳:

恆從小奚奴，騎距驢，背一古破錦囊，遇有所得，即書投囊中。及暮歸，太夫人使婢受囊出之，見所書多，輒曰，是兒要當嘔出心乃已爾。上燈與食，長吉從婢取書，研墨疊紙足成之，投他囊中。

He would always go off riding a donkey followed by a young Xi slave. On his back he carried an old tattered brocade bag. If he happened to get something, he would write it down at once and throw it in the bag. When he went back in the evening, his mother had a serving girl take the bag and empty out its contents, and when she saw how much he had written, his mother burst out with: "This boy won't stop until he has spit out his heart." Then she lit the lamps and gave him his dinner. Li He next had the serving girl get what he had written; then grinding ink and taking piles of paper, he would complete them, at which point he would throw them into another bag.[4]

---

[4] Ye Congqi 葉蔥奇, ed., *Li He shiji* 李賀詩集 (Beijing: Renmin wenxue chubanshe, 1980), p. 358.

The differences in these two accounts of composition mark a basic watershed in poetics. Han Yu follows in the mainstream of Confucian poetics, in which the text "spills out of the heart" and gives immediate access to the person within, in Han's case a person shaped by the internalization of ancient values. Han Yu's sense of belatedness forces him to acknowledge the historical mediation of language in the expression of self, leading to the discourse of purification and taking possession of what is "one's own" through the exclusion of others, *ren zhi shuo/yue zhe* 人之說者. Once such purification is achieved, pure immediacy can be restored.[5]

The description of Li He's compositional practice is in the lineage of Tang technical poetics, where the poem begins with a quest for a *trouvaille*, a lucky find. The pseudo–Wang Changling essay "On Literary Conceptions" 論文意 (eighth century) in *Bunkyō hifuron* 文鏡秘府論 offers much advice about letting the mind roam free in the cosmos and such, but it also adds the following:

凡詩人夜間床頭，明置一盞燈。若睡來任睡，睡覺即起，興發意生，精神清爽，了了明白，皆須身在意中。

> Every poet will place an oil lamp by his bed at night for light. If you go to sleep, then let yourself sleep; but if you awaken, get right up. Inspiration appears and conceptions come, and your spirit will be vigorous, clear, and possessed of a wondrous clarity, for it is always necessary that there be [the poet's] physical presence in the conceptions.[6]

---

[5] Bai Juyi's descriptions of his own acts of poetic composition belong to the same tradition (see pp. 18–19, 104–5 above). Both writers acknowledge the mediation of prior literary usage. Han Yu enjoins writers to purge their work of "worn-out words," and Bai Juyi takes pride in his clumsy diction and off rhymes (22069). For both writers authenticity is achieved by violating norms of contemporary usage and confirmed by the mockery of ordinary people. Bai Juyi differs, however, in his strenuous claims of innocent immediacy, and his stylized wildness would prove the more influential model for later writers.

[6] Wang Liqi 王利器, ed., *Wenjing mifulun jiaozhu* 文鏡秘府論校注 (Beijing: Zhongguo shehuike chubanshe, 1983), p. 290. The final clause begins an argument on the organic link between person and poem.

and again later:

> 凡神不安，令人不暢無興。無興即任睡，睡大養神。常須夜停
> 燈任自覺，不須強起。強起即惛迷，所覽無益。紙筆墨常須隨
> 身，興來即錄。若無筆紙，羈旅之間，意多草草。舟行之後，即
> 須安眠。眠足之後，固多清景，江山滿懷，合而生興，須屏絕事
> 務，專任情興。因此，若有制作，皆奇逸。看興稍歇，且如詩未
> 成，待後有興成，卻必不得強傷神。

Whenever the spirit is not at rest, it causes a person to be unrelaxed and lack inspiration. If you lack inspiration, then let yourself go to sleep right away; sleep greatly nurtures spirit. You should always put out the lamp at night and let yourself wake up naturally, but you should not force yourself to get up. If you force yourself to get up, you will be groggy, and you'll get nothing out of whatever you look over. You should always have paper, pen, and ink with you, so that when inspiration comes, you can write it down immediately. If you lack pen and paper, as on a journey, your conceptions will usually be hasty and confused. After a journey by boat, you should sleep peacefully right away; when you have slept enough, you can be certain that many clear scenes of mountains and rivers will fill your feelings, which will merge to generate inspiration; you should block out all practical worries and give yourself over entirely to feelings and inspiration. In this way whatever composition you produce will always be remarkable and untrammeled. If you note that the inspiration is ebbing somewhat before the poem is completed, wait until later when the inspiration comes fully, but you should not harm your spirit by forcing it.[7]

We are not yet in the Mid-Tang world of "getting" couplets; what the poet awaits is "inspiration," *xing* 興, but in the wonderfully practical terms of this passage we already see expressed the form of anticipating what can only come by chance. The anxiety here is not of contamination but of losing what one finds; thus the poet must be rested and ready. This and much else in "On Literary Conceptions" promises techniques for finding something that transcends technique.

---

[7] Ibid., p. 306.

The key term in the Li He biography and in many ninth-century texts on composition is to "get," *de* 得, something. Han Yu uses the more active phrase "to seize (or choose) something in the mind," *qu yu xin* 取於心, which then comes pouring forth through the hand. *De* is very different, more fortuitous than willful. What a poet "gets" may be something imperfect and fragmentary, requiring revision and completion. Han Yu's acts of critical reflection on his earlier texts are done not with an eye to polishing them, but rather to evaluate how far he is along the path to purified identity. Han is looking forward to the time when perfection will come immediately. For Li He, in contrast, the poetic text is always a two-stage affair, which finds tangible embodiment in the two bags. There is the first bag for the staged and anticipated *trouvaille*; then there is the second bag for a retrospective craft that works the *trouvaille* into a poem.

We should pay special attention to the staging of composition in the Li He anecdote, and particularly to the intervention of the women and servants in the household, who are there to help him spit out his heart. Han Yu controls what he is doing; Li He is presented as something like a poetic machine that needs constant attention. The women and servants provide him all the necessary props, and the biography goes on to say that he did this every day, unless he was too drunk or in mourning, suggesting a regularity and routine of production that is indeed machinelike. Like Han Yu, Li He's mother imagines composition as disgorging, but in contrast to the floodlike liquidity of Han Yu's product, Li He's products suggest small and hard nuggets.

In the ninth century a long history of conceptualizing poetic praxis came to the surface and challenged older notions of Confucian poetics. Rather than being a pure manifestation of the poet's "sentiments," *qing* 情, "aims," *zhi* 志, or identity, the poem became a combination of good fortune and craft. The point where this change appeared most clearly was in representing the duration of composition: in earlier poetics the poem's authority depended on its being a direct product of the occasioning moment. We assume that Du Fu wrote his poems about the An Lushan Rebellion immediately following the occasions to which the poems refer. If we surrender that assumption, then the dating of much classical poetry and the biographical inferences drawn from it fall to pieces.[8] In the Mid-Tang, however, there appears an alternative possibility of an extended phase of composition, especially at the level of the line and parallel couplet. If we suppose that Du Fu's poems on the An Lushan Rebellion were completed a decade later in Kuizhou, then this would change the way Du Fu is read. If we suppose that Mid-Tang craftsmen-poets like Li He or Jia Dao 賈島 (779–843) completed poems, even occasional poems, over the span of many years, no reader would be surprised.[9]

The technical theory in "On Literary Conceptions" of *Bunkyō hifuron* already assumes an interval between experience and composition: in place of the immediacy of "stirring and response," there is something closer to Wordsworth's "recollection in tranquillity," allowing that the moment of recollection follows soon after the experience. In the passage quoted earlier we read: "After a journey by boat, you should sleep peacefully right away; when you have slept enough, you can be certain that many clear scenes of mountains and rivers will fill your feelings, which will merge to generate inspiration; you should block out all practical worries and give

---

[8] I speak merely of conventional assumptions in reading; I make no judgment whether such assumptions are historically accurate.

[9] Much is made of Du Fu's reference to revising poems in the seventh "Release from Ennui," 解悶 (11576): "Done with revising recent poems, I chant them long to myself" 新詩改罷自長吟. Here, however, we should note that these are explicitly *recent* poems. We might contrast the final couplet of "Middle Age" 中年 by the late ninth-century poet Zheng Gu 鄭谷 (37469): "Growing slow and frail, I take delight in increasing my study of poetry, / again I take some earlier pieces and revise a few couplets" 衰遲自喜添詩學，更把前題改數聯. Zheng Gu's "earlier pieces" suggests poems that are not very recent. Rather than completing poems as Du Fu does, Zheng Gu sees his poems as things that can be continually revised, a process that is part of perfecting the "study of poetry."

yourself over entirely to feelings and inspiration." The occasion of composition here is not immediate experience (which can produce works that are hasty and confused), but a re-envisagement, a scene of the mind from which all practical considerations have been purged. We are well on our way to acknowledging that the scenes represented in poetry are not those of the everyday world, even when the poem purports to present the particulars of lived experience.

If the poem no longer represents the experience of the senses, then what criteria determine the terms of representation? When writing on a particular occasion, can one write of a bird in the sky even if there actually was no bird in the sky? In a poem composed "on the spot" such deviation from experience might be troubling, but if a poem takes shape over the course of months, years, or decades, such details can become irrelevant.[10] It was already an open secret that the words of the poem were determined as much by parallelism, tonal requirements, euphony, and decorum as by the occasioning situation. If a poetic scene is envisaged, then why shouldn't its details be chosen for greatest effect?

In this context it is appropriate to quote the most famous anecdote about poetic craft in the Chinese tradition, the anecdote that provided the classical language with its standard term for finely considered aesthetic decisions, *tuiqiao* 推敲, literally "shove-knock." The following version of the anecdote is from He Guangyuan's 何光遠 *Jianjie lu* 鑒戒錄 from the Five Dynasties. The anecdote concerns the early ninth century poet Jia Dao.

忽一日於驢上吟得「鳥宿池邊樹，僧敲月下門」初欲著推字，或欲著敲字，煉之未定，遂于驢上作推字手勢，又作敲自手勢。不覺行半坊。觀者訝之，島似不見。時韓吏部愈權京尹，意氣清嚴威振紫陌。經第三對呵唱，島但手勢未已。俄為官者推下驢，擁

---

[10] This is not an issue in Western poetics, but it was important in traditional Chinese poetics. Writers of "remarks on poetry," *shihua* 詩話, took a particular delight in pointing out factual errors, which were considered a serious blemish on the poem.

至尹前，島方覺悟。顧問欲責之。島具對「偶得一聯，吟安一字
未定，神游詩府，致衝大官，非敢取尤，希垂至鑒」。韓立馬良
久思之，謂島曰「作敲字佳矣」。

One day, all at once, while riding on his mule, he came up
with the verse: "The bird spends the night in the tree by the
pool, / the monk knocks at the gate under the moonlight." At
first he wanted to use the word "shove"; then he wanted to
use the word "knock." Not having settled on the best usage,
he rode along on his mule, first drawing the character
"shove" with his hand, then drawing the character "knock."
Without realizing it, he passed through half a city ward in
this fashion. Those who observed him were astonished, but
Jia Dao seemed not to see them. At the time Han Yu held
power as the Metropolitan Governor of the capital; Han had
a stern and punctilious disposition, and his awesome presence at that moment made itself felt on the great avenue.
[His attendants] repeatedly shouted at Jia Dao to get out of
the way, but he just went on writing characters with his
hand. Only when all of a sudden he was pushed down from
his mule by officials and dragged before the Metropolitan
Governor did Jia Dao realize the situation. The advisors
wanted to have him reprimanded, but Jia Dao responded, "I
just happened now to get a couplet, but I haven't been able
to get a particular word right. My spirit was wandering in the
realm of poetry, and this is what led me to run into Your Ex-
cellency. I do not dare call your wrath down upon me, but I
hope you might be kind enough to give this some considera-
tion." Han Yu halted his horse, thought about it for a while,
and said to Jia Dao, " 'Knock' is finer."[11]

Although we cannot trace this anecdote to the ninth
century (much less make a judgment regarding its historical
accuracy), it perfectly represents the new concern with poetic
craft and the admiration for the poet's deliberative absorption
that took shape in the early ninth century. Craft and helpless
compulsion are unified in the figure of the poet wandering the
streets of the capital in a daze.

[11] Wang Dapeng 王大鵬 et al., eds., *Zhongguo lidai shihua xuan* 中國
歷代詩話選 (Changsha: Yuelu shushe, 1985), pp. 118–19.

We do not know if the couplet Jia Dao "got" was supposed to have been re-envisaged or invented; we do not know if the couplet was supposed to belong to a poem in process or the poem was to be supplied later, to frame the couplet. The couplet today is found in a poem entitled "On Li Ning's Secluded Dwelling" 題李凝幽居, but we do not know when the anecdote above supposedly occurred in relation to Jia Dao's visit to Li Ning's hermitage. It is clear, however, that the criterion for choosing the right word belonged to poetic craft rather than to referential accuracy. This provoked the fury of the great seventeenth-century critic Wang Fuzhi 王夫之. In *Jiangzhai's Remarks on Poetry* 薑齋詩話, Wang Fuzhi took special aim at the implications of this anecdote.

「僧敲月下門」祇是妄想揣摩，如說他人夢，縱令形容酷似，何嘗毫髮關心？知然者，以其沈吟推敲二字，就他作想也。若即景會心，則或推或敲，必居其一，因景因情，自然靈妙，何勞擬議哉？

"The monk knocks at the gate beneath the moon" is nothing more than mere guessing, false speculation, as if trying to describe someone else's dream. Even if the description seems very lifelike, it doesn't truly touch the heart in the least. Those who understand this will recognize that brooding over the choice between "push" and "knock" is mere speculation on behalf of some other. But if the scene meets mind, then it may be "push" or it may be "knock," but it will have to be one or the other: since it will follow from scene and follow from state of mind, the line will be naturally numinous and subtle. There will be none of the bother of debating the right choice.[12]

Or to put it in crassly empirical terms, if the couplet is true, then the poet will know whether the monk (Jia Dao himself) pushed or knocked. For Wang Fuzhi, to be "genuine," *zhen* 眞, the poetic scene must be referentially accurate (although

---

[12] Wang Fuzhi 王夫之, *Jiangzhai shihua jianzhu* 薑齋詩話注, ed. with commentary by Dai Hongsen 戴鴻森 (Beijing: Renmin wenxue chubanshe, 1981), p. 52.

referential accuracy is not, in itself, a guarantee of genuineness).

The "heart" that Li He's mother feared he would spit up is the craftsman's heart. The poet goes out riding his donkey *in order to* compose poetry; the poems do not come of themselves as an integral part of a life whose center is elsewhere. The brocade bag is always there to receive whatever he "gets."

Images of obsession, absorption, and even possession by the "poetry imp," *shimo* 詩魔, became commonplace in the ninth century.[13] The laughter and amazement of others are noted as a source of pride. In ostensibly ridiculing himself, the poet praises himself.

> Xue Neng 薛能 (ca. 817–?),
> *Lampooning Myself* 自諷 (30950)

千題萬詠過三旬，忘食貪魔作瘦人。
行處便吟君莫笑，就中詩病不任春。

> In a thousand themes, ten thousand verses
>   I've passed these thirty days,
> I forget meals: the imp of greed
>   has made me a gaunt man
> If I chant a verse wherever I go,
>   do not laugh at me!—
> in the midst of my poetry disease
>   I cannot bear the spring.

Xue Neng's third line would immediately recall one of the most famous quatrains of the eighth century, Wang Han's 王翰 "Liangzhou Lyric" 涼州詞 (07557):

葡萄美酒夜光杯，欲飲琵琶馬上催。
醉臥沙場君莫笑，古來征戰幾人回。

> Sweet wine of the grape,
>   cup of phosphorescent jade,
> at the point of drinking, mandolins play
>   on horseback, urging us on.
> If I lie down drunk in the desert,
>   do not laugh at me!—

[13] Cf. 20740.

men have marched to battle from long ago,
and how many ever returned?

The historical transformation to the figure provoking laughter is significant: in place of the drunken wildness of fear and despair of the soldier going off to war, we find the poet in the grip of the "disease of poetry." The figure of the soldier belongs to a world where behavior is intelligible in terms of motives and moods common to all; the risible poet's madness is presented as singular and inexplicable, a mark of his distinction from ordinary humanity.

As noted in the preceding essay, Bai Juyi also refers to poetry as an "addiction," *pi* 癖, and a disease, *bing* 病.[14] In this interest in poetry as somatic compulsion, we have a significant contrast with Meng Jiao, the oldest of the Mid-Tang poets, for whom disease also played an insistent role in his discussion of poetry. For Meng Jiao sickness was the physical and cosmic condition from which he claimed to write. As *kuyin* 苦吟, "bitter chanting," transformed from the pain that occasioned writing to the pains taken in writing itself, so the figure of disease ceased to be the circumstance of poetry and came instead to qualify poetry and the poet's compositional process. These ninth-century transformations of images of composition are still organic: indeed, all these figures serve to stress the involuntary, bodily compulsion in writing poetry. Poetic compulsion is, however, restricted to a select few, "poets," who find their alienation from common experience to be a virtue.

A number of interesting consequences follow from this separation of poetry from common experience. Several of these can be seen in a polite poem of gratitude by the early ninth-century poet Yao He 姚合.

---

[14] See pp. 104–5 above. For Bai Juyi, however, somatic compulsion produces the extreme of artlessness rather than the extreme of artfulness.

Delightedly Perusing a Scroll of Poems
by Censor Lu of Jingzhou
喜覽涇州盧侍御詩卷 (26835)

新詩十九首，麗格出青冥。
得處神應駭，成時力盡停。
正愁聞更喜，沈醉見還醒。
自是天才健，非關筆硯靈。

Your recent poems, nineteen in all, possess
a sumptuous style that comes from dark
    heavens.
When you got something, spirit was surely
    amazed;
when completed, your force stopped entirely.
In melancholy, hearing them restores
    delight;
if deeply drunk, reading them sobers one
    again.
It is the vigor of natural talent by itself
and has nothing to do with magic of inkstone
    or brush.

We might first note the thrill of composition. The second
couplet economically recapitulates the two stages of composition in the anecdote about Li He and gives us an even clearer
indication of the nature of the *trouvaille*. If the spirit is
amazed on "getting" something, then the particular poetic
gem found is unforeseen—something reached with the aid of
Heaven, as the commonplace had it. The words of the poem
are no longer mere self-expression, but a surprising acquisition. The next phase, which brings acquisition to completion
(Li He's second bag), involves the expenditure of "effort" or
"force," *li* 力, a process that does lie within the realm of conscious action.

The capacity of the poetic *trouvaille* to amaze the poet
finds a counterpart in the poem's affect in the world at large.
Usually poetic affect had been described either as the reader
understanding how the poet felt, the circumstances that
stirred him to composition, or as "sympathetic response" in
the technical sense, in which the reader is moved by the

poem because his own disposition or mood resonates with that of the poem or poet.[15] Here, however, the poem continues to surprise and has the power to reverse the disposition of the reader, transforming melancholy to delight and drunkenness to sobriety. This poetry is no longer a mere extension of the poet's self; it is an autonomous force.

The question remains where the poem comes from. Yao He rejects anecdotes of magic inkstones and brushes as the source of the poem's power (perhaps all who write make a fetish of certain writing implements being imbued with particularly efficacious virtue). Yao He gives a double answer, but one whose alternatives can easily be reconciled. Lu's style comes from Heaven and from an innate talent that is granted by Heaven (translated as "natural" in the seventh line).

Remarkably, the amazing *trouvaille* can be conceptualized as having been found within the self. This moment, when the writer finds things within himself of which he was not aware, is a primitive idea of the unconscious. In "Conjectures on Original Composition" (1759), Edward Young represents this with the metaphor of diving into the sea, followed by the emergence of a sun.

> Therefore dive deep into thy bosom; learn the depth, extent, bias, and full fort of thy mind; contract full intimacy with the stranger within thee; excite and cherish every spark of intellectual light and heat, however smothered under former negligence, or scattered through the dull dark mass of common thoughts; and collecting them into a body, let thy genius rise (if a genius thou hast) as the sun from chaos; and if I should then say, like an *Indian, Worship it,* (though too bold) yet should I say little more than my second rule enjoins, (*viz.*) *Reverence thyself.*[16]

Instead of being found in an ocean, in "A Whimsy, Presented to a Friend" 戲贈友人 (31515), Jia Dao conceptualizes

---

[15] The major exception here is functional Confucian poetics in which the poem awakens moral sentiments in the reader.

[16] James Harry Smith and Edd Winfield Parks, eds., *The Great Critics*, 3d ed. (New York: Norton, 1951), p. 422.

these "sparks of intellectual light and heat" as submerged in a well. The writer need not dive; he need only use a well rope.

一旦不作詩，心源如廢井。
筆硯爲轆轤，吟詠作縻綆。
朝來重汲引，依舊得清冷。
書贈同懷人，詞中多苦辛。

One morning I wrote no poems,
the mind-source seemed like an abandoned well.
Brush and inkstone are the well pulley,
chanting serves as the well rope.
Since dawn I drew from it repeatedly,
as always what I get is cold and clear.
I write it out for one who feels as I do:
in the phrases, much bitter pain.

Young dives; Han Yu gushes; and Jia Dao must drop his speculative bucket, which may, despite the effort, come up dry. The division between the active, conscious self and that which is accessible but hidden within the self finds a peculiar echo in the division between the ostensibly "whimsical" tone of the poem and the "bitter pain" of the poetic lines recovered from the well. Nor can we tell if the "bitter pain" is the poet's general state of mind or "painstaking" efforts in composition. Does the friend share the poet's misery, or is his like-mindedness found in his sensibility to appreciate the "painstaking" efforts? In what sense is this playful?

The poetic *trouvaille* is transposed beneath the surface of what is immediately apparent; the poet "gets" an image, a line, or a couplet and is amazed. The displacement of the perfect line or couplet to an accessible "beyond" is structurally repeated in formulations of the poetic image that were taking shape in the same period. Those who have written on Tang poetics have generally concentrated on the development of the idea of the "transcendent image." I use the term "transcendent" with some discomfort, but advisedly, since the central characteristic is its being "beyond," either "beyond image," *xiangwai* 象外, or "beyond words," *yanwai* 言外. Especially in the formulation "beyond image," *xiangwai*, let me call this a "transmimetic" theory.[17] The late ninth-century critic Sikong Tu 司空圖 (837–908) described this as "image beyond image" and "scene beyond scene," a liminally envisaged presence described by a metaphor that Sikong Tu attributed to the late eighth-century poet Dai Shulun 戴叔倫: "The scene given by a poet is like the sun being warm on Indigo Fields and the fine jade there giving off a mist—you can gaze on but you can't fix in your eyes."[18] Dai Shulun uses the figure of mists to make sharply defined visual presences liminal, and mist was to become an important part of the "poetic."

A parent of the elusive poetic image can be found in a remarkable passage in "On Literary Conceptions" in *Bunkyō hifuron*. This passage acknowledges a disjunction between empirical experience and compositional praxis (as opposed to the involuntary immediacy of "stirring and response"), along with one of the clearest statements of reflection theory in the Chinese theoretical tradition.

夫置意作詩，即須凝心，目擊其物，便以心擊之，深穿其境。如登高山絕頂，下臨萬象，如在掌中。以此見象，心中了見，當此即用。如無有不似，仍以律調之定，然後書之於紙，會其題目。山林、日月、風景爲眞，以歌詠之，猶如水中見日月，文章是景物色是本，照之須了見其 象也。

When one has an idea to write a poem, one must immediately concentrate the mind; when the eye strikes upon the thing, then one must let the mind strike upon it and penetrate deeply into its world-scene [*jing*, perhaps "environment"]. It is like climbing to the highest peak of a mountain and looking down on the thousands of images as if in the palm of one's hand. When one sees the images in this way, they are fully revealed in mind, and at this point they may be used [in a poem]. If everything resembles [the original], one goes on to determine the sound patterns, and only then

---

[17] Since the term "image" (*xiang* 象) involves categorical "resemblance" (*xiang* 像), a poetic quality that is "beyond image" is one in which the essentially poetic quality lies beyond representational verisimilitude.

[18] Stephen Owen, *Readings in Chinese Literary Thought* (Cambridge, Mass.: Harvard University Press, 1992), p. 357.

can you write it down on paper, comprehending the topic in the title. Mountain forests or the sun and moon or the scene are genuine; and when one sings about them in a poem, it is like seeing the sun and moon in the water. The literary work is the reflection and the colors of physical things are the original. When you catch the reflection, you must let the image be fully revealed.[19]

The passage begins with the author's reiteration of the priority of the poetic "idea" or "conception" (*yi* 意), and a poetic meditation to follow it. This probably corresponds to "comprehending the topic in the title," *hui qi timu* 會其題目, later in the passage (perhaps related to examination poetry and compositional pedagogy in which a poet is called upon to write on a set topic). But the passage shifts immediately to experiential composition. First the eyes see something, and then the mind sets to work on it. What is experienced is a world-scene, *jing* 境, comprising "thousands of images," which are grasped as a totality and in miniature ("as if in the palm of one's hand"). The miniaturization that occurs in this comprehensive grasp anticipates the mimetic figure of reflection later. That envisaged grasp of the whole must exist before verbal composition. The poetic text is then described quite explicitly as the "reflection" of the genuine (*zhen* 眞) world, in which the envisaged poetic scene becomes the transparent mediator between text and real world.

We have here a fully developed notion of a "poetic scene" in the mind, mediating between experience and composition, which will become an important assumption in later poetics. But the perfect correspondence between the "original" and the reflection here can be taken as the ground against which to understand the development of the aesthetics of "beyond images," *xiangwai* 象外. That is, here in popular poetics we find the missing mimetic theory (of a sort very different from the earlier "clever similitude," *qiaosi* 巧似), that we would assume

[19] Wang Liqi, *Wenjing mifulun jiaozhu*, p. 285. Although *jing* 景 may be translated as "scene," in this context, surrounded by terms of mirroring and reflection, it seems best to read it as *ying*, a "reflection."

to find as the possibility negated in the "transmimetic" *xiang-wai*. As we will see, the transmimetic representation becomes associated with the poetic *trouvaille* that is *not* based in empirical experience.

Dai Shulun, Sikong Tu's authority for the transmimetic scene, was a poet of the second half of the eighth century and a rough contemporary of the poet and critic Jiaoran 皎然 (730–99). Although the basis of a poetics in which poetry's value lies "beyond" something can be found earlier, its first clear statement occurs in Jiaoran's "Statutes of Poetry" 詩式, commenting on the famous touchstone line of the fifth-century poet Xie Lingyun 謝靈運: "Pool and pond grow with spring plants," *chitang sheng chuncao* 池塘生春草. Jiaoran identifies this section by quoting two of Xie Lingyun's most famous lines:

「池塘生春草」「明月照積雪」
　評曰：客有問予，謝公此二句優劣奚若。余因引梁征遠將軍記室鐘嶸評爲隱，秀之語，且鐘生旣非詩人，安可輒議。徒欲聾瞽後來耳目。且如「池塘生春草」，情在言外；「明月照積雪」，旨冥句中。風力雖齊，取興各別。〔中略〕情者如康樂公「池塘生春草」是也。抑由情在言外，故其辭似淡而無味，常手覽之，何異文侯聽古樂哉。謝氏傳曰，吾嘗在永嘉西堂作詩，夢見惠連，因得「池塘生春草」。豈非神助乎？

"Pool and pond grow with spring plants"

"The bright moon shines on drifts of snow"

The judgment: Someone asked me my opinion on which of these two lines by Xie Lingyun was the better. I then cited the judgment of Zhong Rong, the Record Keeper of the Liang General of Far Campaigns, who took them as [examples of] "latent" (*yin*) and "outstanding" (*xiu*) diction, respectively; yet since Zhong Rong was no poet himself, how could he so rashly offer an opinion? All he wanted to do was deafen the ears and blind the eyes of those who came after him. In the case of "Pool and pond grow with spring plants," the feeling lies beyond the words; in the case of "The bright moon shines on drifts of snow," the import is mysteriously within the line. Although their affective power is equal, each is distinct in the kind of stirring it chooses. . . . As for [poems showing] feeling, Xie's "Pool and pond grow with spring plants," is an example of such; it comes from feeling lying beyond the words, thus the phrases seem bland and lacking in flavor; and if someone ordinary reads it over, it is no different from Count Wen [of Wei] listening to the ancient music [who said it made him worry lest he fall asleep]. The "Biography of Mr. Xie" says, "I was writing poems in the Western Hall at Yongjia and saw Xie Huilian in a dream; it was then I got 'Pool and pond grow with spring plants.'" Isn't this an obvious case of spirit aid?[20]

To at least some degree, Jiaoran is appealing to "feeling lying beyond the words" to explain why such a simple line should be so beautiful. As phrases often do, however, "feeling lying beyond the words" took on a life of its own, generating implications beyond the occasioning motive.

"Pool and pond grow with spring plants" remained a touchstone of the ineffably "poetic," especially for Wang Fuzhi, who so deeply objected to the artifice of any line or couplet not based on empirical experience. Yet this quintessentially "poetic" line was not supposed to have come from an experience of the world but from Xie Lingyun's dream encounter with his cousin Xie Huilian. In Zhong Rong's (ca. 465–518) account in the *Grades of Poetry* 詩品, Xie Lingyun *cheng* 成, "completed" or "produced," the line out of the dream.[21] In Jiaoran's significant rephrasing, Xie Lingyun "got," *de* 得, the line. Moreover, in his retelling of the occasion, Jiaoran omitted the final clause in Zhong Rong's version: Xie Lingyun is supposed to have said, "There is a spirit's aid in these words; *they are not my words*" (italics mine).[22] The ineffably poetic image, the paradigmatic image that lies "beyond" the referential value of the words, was a *trouvaille*,

[20] Li Zhuangying 李壯鷹, ed., *Shishi jiaozhu* 詩式校注 (Ji'nan: Qi Lu shushe, 1987), pp. 115–16.

[21] Zhong Rong's judgment regarding the authorship of the line may be implied in his inclusion of the anecdote in his comments on Xie Huilian rather than those on Xie Lingyun.

[22] Chen Yanjie 陳延傑, ed., *Shipin zhu* 詩品注 (Beijing: Renmin wenxue chubanshe, 1961), p. 46.

something whose value is guaranteed by the fact that it comes from beyond the poet and his conscious capacities. The role of sleep is significant, in many ways corresponding to the automatic, machinelike quality of Li He's poetic production. The *Bunkyō hifuron* advises the poet that poems will come to you if you sleep, and Xie Lingyun's most famous line comes in a dream. This is as close as the Chinese tradition comes to the vatic idea of the poet, the poet as conduit for "spirit aid."

In the passage from Jiaoran's "Statutes of Poetry," the touchstone poetic line of Xie Lingyun has *no* basis in lived experience—indeed in Zhong Rong's version, it is explicitly not even Xie Lingyun's own line. We are moving toward a new notion of poetry in which the scene is not "seen" but entirely "envisioned." Furthermore, what is envisioned is not a poem, but a line or a couplet, or even a "poetic idea," that exists before its linguistic expression. Around this core of envisagement a poem is built—to use Li Shangyin's term to describe the practice of Li He, *zucheng* 足成, literally "made adequate and complete." The central term of value for such envisaged scenes is that they are "beyond" the definite and merely empirical, whether words or image or scene.

We see something of the relation between the elusively "poetic" scene and the verbal object in a famous passage from Liu Yuxi's "Account of the Wuling Collection of Mr. Dong" 董氏武陵集紀:

詩者其文章之蘊邪，義得而言喪，故微而難能；境生於象外，故精而寡和。千里之繆，不容秋毫。

Is not poetry the most "intensive" [*yun*] form of writing? When its truth is gotten, the words perish, thus it is subtle and hard to be skillful at. A scene-world is generated beyond the images, thus it is the refined essence with which few can harmonize. A divergence of a thousand leagues lies in less than the space of an autumn hair.[23]

---

[23] Qu Tuiyuan 瞿蛻園, ed., *Liu Yuxi ji jianzheng* 劉禹錫集箋證 (Shanghai: Shanghai guji chubanshe, 1989), p. 517.

In the passage from "On Literary Conceptions," we saw how the envisaged scene preceded composition in words. Here we see how reading the words leads back to envisagement (some homology between reading and composition is one of the most enduring characteristics of the Chinese theoretical tradition). Just as a mist blurs the sharp and definite edges of things in Dai Shulun's formulation of the "poetic," Liu Yuxi here has the poetic scene effacing the words that produced it (echoing Zhuangzi). The poem is the "most intensive form of writing" *wenzhang zhi yun* 文章之蘊. *Yun*, which I have translated as "intensive," means that it has much "stored" within it; it is "replete." Reading seems to release the compacted contents, obliterating the verbal package. "Beyond the words" is here also "after the words."

In attaining the quality of the envisaged "scene-world generated beyond images," *jing sheng yu xiangwai* 境生於象外, we find a singularity that excludes others ("few can harmonize"). The figure of the poem's singular perfection is one of a journey, in which a hair's breadth difference of direction at the beginning will lead to immense difference when the goal is attained. Quietly here, we are being told about the difference between the true poet and the versifier. All begin very close, but the product of the true poet is separated from mere verse by a thousand leagues. And the essential difference is precisely in achieving transmimetic envisagement.

As we have seen, at the turn of the ninth century the poet was becoming a figure apart; in the same way poetry was being given a special status, with hints of a radical difference between poetry and mere verse. It is only a short distance to one of the most remarkable statements about poetry in the ninth century, a line from a poem by Du Mu (28214):

浮世除詩盡強名。

In this world adrift, except in poems,
   all words are forced on things.

"Words forced [on things]," *qiangming* 強名, is a phrase

from the *Laozi*, where the word "Way" is forced on something that has no name. Quite simply Du Mu is claiming here that poetry is the only true language. And the truth of such language, what makes it adequate, is the production of scenes that are "beyond words" and "beyond image."

❖

Romance

The Mid-Tang saw the rise of a culture of romance, with the representation of individually chosen and socially unauthorized relationships between men and women.[1] The rise of romance is closely related to the development of individual acts of interpretation or valuation and the demarcation of private space. Romance imaginatively institutes a minimal society of election, at once located within a world of social determination yet protected from it by the mutual absorption of the lovers. Narratives of romance go further to explore the conflict that must follow from the attempt to institute such an autonomous domain within the social whole.

In romance as in the private life of the garden, moreover, representations cannot be entirely dissociated from attitudes and behavior. The circulation of poems shaped leisure activities, invited the construction of miniature ponds, and encouraged new poems to celebrate the experience. In the same way discursive images of romance, circulating in elite urban society and the demimonde,[2] came to seem a real possibility;

[1] "Romance" here is used in its popular, rather than its technical literary sense, though the term is appropriate in locating the large human phenomenon in discourse.

[2] The use of the term "demimonde" deserves some comment. I use it to refer to women, usually of entertainer or merchant background (that is, socially inferior to the Confucian elite), who had relatively free contact with men. If an affection developed, such women could generally be taken into concubinage. I intend the term to refer to a gray area, between prostitution and the guarded respectability of elite households.

and although we cannot know with any certainty if Mid-Tang lovers felt the passions and had the experiences that the poems and stories describe, we do know that others, not themselves lovers, believed this to be the case.

The problem of romance is the "happily ever after." The speculative institution of a relationship, both within the romance narrative and probably within the social culture of romance, is initially identical to the construction of a narrative; that is, the lovers and those who assist them stage the relationship, emplotting it in the same way the author does. But whereas romance itself is a free choice to move to a state of permanent bliss, literary narrative, by contrast, must conclude and thus may act to limit freedom and disrupt bliss.

We come back to boundary conditions, the power to enclose and protect a space. The poet's ability to create a protected, private, domestic space was predicated on his assertion of its smallness and superfluity. Romance is an attempt to close off a more serious domain as private space, and, in doing so, it comes into conflict with the vital interests of the social whole. Here the boundaries of enclosure are usually broken; the outside world intrudes and lays claim to the protagonists.[3]

Balances of free choice and compulsion play an important role in the romance narrative, as they do in all Mid-Tang attempts to represent spheres of autonomy. The internal compulsion of the lover's passion and the external compulsion of family, state, or circumstance all can be represented directly in romance; indeed, autonomy may be no more than the disputed territory between such opposing compulsions. There is, however, one significant form of external compulsion that must be repressed in order for romance to exist. Traces and shadows of this particular external compulsion continue to break into the narrative representations of romance. This is

---

[3] Romances in which the couple lives "happily ever after" usually require an immortal rather than a mortal demimondaine. In order to achieve a mortal "happily ever after," the Tang tale "Li Wa's Story" must elaborately integrate the former demimondaine into family and state.

financial compulsion, the social fact that permitted the demi-monde, the site of romance, to exist. Negating financial compulsion in the woman's relation to the man is an essential plot element in many romance narratives, whether it is Huo Xiaoyu spending her own money, Li Wa breaking with her mother and using up her savings ("Li Wa's Story" 李娃傳), or Mrs. Wang's continuing her vigil for Li Zhangwu beyond the grave ("Li Zhangwu's Story" 李章武傳). In each of these fictional cases, the representation of a relationship transcends financial dependency on the part of the woman.

This particular plot element should remind us of the difference between a fiction of romance and the social realities of the demimonde, the context to which fictions of romance referred. Liaisons in the demimonde were supported by financial transactions. The display of affection on the part of the woman was always called into question by the financial nature of the exchange and the inequality of power involved. The power of financial compulsion to disrupt the appearance of blissful affection is demonstrated very powerfully in the first half of "Li Wa's Story," where the "mother" forces Li Wa to break with the young man once his money is used up. Fictions of an affection (or in the case of Li Wa, a sense of right) that transcends financial dependency served an important structural role in the culture of romance, guaranteeing the mutuality of free election, which was the ideal on which the culture of romance depended and which separated it from mere sexual commerce.[4]

One should also note the general suppression of representations of the financial dependency of the young man (though this too is violently exposed in "Li Wa's Story" and played out in an open and intricate way in "Ren's Story" 任氏傳). In "Li Wa's Story" and "Huo Xiaoyu's Story" 霍小玉傳, the young man comes to the capital with a certain amount of

---

[4] The fact that Li Wa acts out of a sense of moral obligation rather than love is essential to the ultimate sanctioning of her relationship with the young scholar and her acceptance by the family and state.

substance to support him during a term, after which he is supposed to pass the examination and become self-sufficient. An illusion of the man's independence and financial power is necessary for entering the relationship. This is a variation on the Mid-Tang concern with identity and possession: like possessed territory, autonomy is proved by one's ability to freely dispose of oneself.

Such freely elected relationships that transcend financial dependency suggest a deep awareness of the problem that financial dependency posed for feeling. These Tang stories do not represent the social facts of the demimonde; they represent the culture of the demimonde embodied in fictions that are motivated by its deepest concerns. That is, we have here a simple and forceful example of how fictions represent not a society as it is but a society's interests.

These are texts by men: the stories clearly speak to the anxieties of men to whom genuine feeling on the part of a woman mattered, feeling that might be suspect given the social and economic inequalities. Unlike marriage, in which the woman's position was institutional rather than defined by feeling, the culture of romance depended on a fiction of continuing free choice. In one common plot, a singing girl falls in love with an official, he has to leave, and in one way or another she shows her steadfast devotion even though the lovers have spent only a short period together. In this question of continuation, terms and limits are of central importance: falling out of love, running out of money, being betrayed, dying, having the relationship disrupted by someone more powerful, such as a parent or a powerful competitor who desires the beloved.

We do not know, however, if the audience for stories of romance was exclusively or even predominantly male.[5] The

---

[5] The question of the literacy of women in the demimonde during the Tang, both in degree and extent, is perhaps unanswerable. A number of points, can, however, be observed in regard to women's participation in the Mid-Tang culture of romance. First, some demimondaines such as Xue Tao and Li Jilan (as well as Yu Xuanji, if we classify her as

fact that these fictions embody male interests does not pre-
clude the possibility that they also embody the interests of
the women in the demimonde. The continuing devotion of a
man was one pragmatic way out of the demimonde, and a
way "out" of the demimonde in a symbolic sense. The way to
figure one's body not as something sold because of need was
through a fiction of election that transcended financial dependency.

Stories from the Mid-Tang culture of romance differ in
significant ways from earlier erotic narratives. An Early Tang
story like "The Cave of Roving Immortals" 遊仙窟 contains the
core formula of many stories, all of which center on the question of putting a limit on an extended erotic relationship. One
or more young men meet one or more young women, usually
in some unfamiliar or marginal space—the grotto, lair, or
tomb, all transformed into the illusion of a sumptuous
dwelling. The young man is held in thrall and enthralled for a
while. If, after a term is done, he escapes that thralldom, then
the woman was a goddess and he feels a sense of elegiac loss.
If he does not escape, the woman is a beast and should be
destroyed. These alternatives by no means exhaust the numerous variations of this simple story.

These versions of the simple story almost always figure
the beloved as a goddess or a were-creature (most commonly
a were-fox) and not as a human demimondaine. Such stories
are figural accounts of unauthorized sexual relations; in
these stories there is no ambiguity regarding the gender
whose interests they address; these are purely male stories.
The young man with surplus capital, translated into surplus
time, spends his substance (uses up his term) until at last he
feels that he has ruined himself spending too much or wishes
he had more to spend.

---

a demimondaine) were literate: we have their poems. Second, in stories
and poems the literacy of demimondaines is often a casual assumption.
Finally, we know that many of the classical tales of romance had ballad
versions, which could clearly have been understood aurally; and these
same stories were certainly retold orally.

Although such simple erotic tales continued to be written, the famous tales of romance of the late eighth and early ninth centuries transform this core story in significant and interesting ways. Economic compulsion and financial dependency run everywhere beneath the surface of these stories, but the surface narrative becomes a theater of choice and different kinds of compulsion. "Ren's Story" is a wonderful example of such a transformation, in which the beast-woman becomes the most human of all demimondaines, caught in a complex drama of financial dependency, trying to balance accounts with the powerful patron and provide financial independence to her lover, the man who wins her because he treats her like a human being with free choice. As stories place greater attention on the woman's freedom of choice, a corresponding change takes place in the representation of the man: male constancy becomes a positive value and an issue. The callous betrayer enters the repertoire of types in romantic narrative.

"Huo Xiaoyu's Story" may be taken as a paradigm of problematic Mid-Tang fictional romance.[6] It begins with the talented young poet Li Yi looking for a suitable companion in the demimonde, seeking a beloved not only as an act of election but also as an act of selection ("election" here means a radical act of choice that involves commitment and extended time; it is the free choice to limit one's freedom of choice). Li Yi takes into his employ the noted procuress Miss Bao, who brings him word of a self-supporting young woman who is looking for an exceptional young man. Her pedigree is described, and it is a suitable match for his own—although her reduced social circumstances make her appropriate for a liaison in the demimonde. This will be the perfect romance in which neither party is financially dependent, and both choose the other freely. Bao has arranged for Li Yi to meet the young woman at noon on the following day at her dwelling place. Indeed, there is an element of comedy as Li Yi suddenly finds himself not only choosing himself but being the object of

---

[6] For a translation of "Huo Xiaoyu's Story," see pp. 178–91.

choice, grooming himself, borrowing a horse and trappings, and anxiously wondering whether he will meet her approval. "As daylight broke, he put on his turban and looked at himself in the mirror, afraid that she wouldn't find him to her liking." This phase, in which the young man anticipates being seen, however, reminds us that "Huo Xiaoyu's Story" belongs to a minority of fictional romances in which report of the other precedes the encounter. It was more common for the lover to catch sight of the beloved by accident, although often within a larger context of seeking a beloved. The moment in which the male protagonist is overcome by a flood of passion on first seeing the beloved is the figure of internal compulsion that counterbalances the element of election in the story of romance. In these opening scenes of "Huo Xiaoyu's Story," however, choice is raised to the level of theme in the only way it can be: as something not-yet-decided. And since the initial "appearance" of a beloved, male or female, is the deciding moment of election, Li Yi anticipates and carefully stages his own appearance.

The element of being seen, and thus judged, is carried into his arrival at Huo Xiaoyu's house. First, the procuress Bao teases him, treating Li Yi's appearance as if it were a trespass, which indeed it would be if Huo Xiaoyu were entirely respectable. This is repeated in the marvelous parrot scene, which even more strongly invokes liminal respectability:

> In the courtyard there were four cherry trees, and from the one in the northwest corner there was hung a cage with a parrot in it. When it saw Li Yi come in, it spoke, "A man is coming—quick, pull down the curtains!" By nature Li Yi was proper and reserved, and his heart was still apprehensive and beset by doubts. When he heard the bird speak out so suddenly, he was overcome with panic and didn't dare go on further.

Li Yi is recognized as an intruder into the women's quarters (by a parrot with the peculiar ability to distinguish sex in human beings), and he shrinks back in panic, as if in the wrong narrative and a social situation where entirely different rules operate. As a result, he must literally be taken by the procuress Bao and Huo Xiaoyu's mother, acting as proxies for Huo Xiaoyu, and brought inside. Here we should recall that one of the determinants of the possession of territory is the ability to exclude others, and hence the power to invite them in by choice. Li Yi is entering woman's space.

His entrance into Huo Xiaoyu's house—however hesitant—is a transgressive act of great significance. One of the most important aspects of the culture of romance is its site. The central ceremony of a "proper" marriage is meeting the bride and bringing her to the groom's home, hence into his family. The women of the demimonde, along with the foxes and goddesses that are their supernatural doubles, receive the men in their own houses, even if the upkeep comes ultimately from the lover. That reversal of the relation between host and guest ("guest" being a term often associated with brides) is part of a set of partial reversals of power that keeps romantic relationships "in play." Note that later, after Li Yi has betrayed Huo Xiaoyu, he does his best to avoid her, and it is of central importance that he be brought to her house to meet her again. Willful and callous outside, once he is back in her house, Li Yi is helpless before her theater of death.

Entering the house for the first time, Li Yi begins the game of politesse and deference that mimics social negotiations in the outside world and, we suspect, was an important part of actual sexual negotiations in the demimonde. These are always figured in terms of marriage negotiations, again with the central difference that consummation and cohabitation occur in the woman's house. The negotiations completed, we have at last the necessary scene of the young woman's "appearance," the dazzling light that conventionally overwhelms the male and makes him lose control of himself.

> Then she [Xiaoyu's mother] ordered that wine and food be served and had Xiaoyu come out from her chamber on the

eastern side of the hall. Li Yi went to greet her, but all he
was aware of was something like an alabaster forest and jade
trees throughout the whole room, casting their dazzling radiance back and forth, and as he turned his gaze, the crystalline rays struck him.

What is remarkable is how thoroughly this is prearranged,
staged, and elaborately negotiated. This initial visual display
imitates and anticipates the display of the body later and the
sexual bliss soon afterward in the story. The contractual negotiations are not supposed to impinge upon the experience of
inner compulsion. In contrast to the conventional expression
of the male's choice of the woman by being overwhelmed, the
woman signals her choice of the male by banter. Reports—
Miss Bao's advertisements of the young man and young
woman to each other—played an essential role in bringing
them together, but now we find that Huo Xiaoyu was also
drawn to Li Yi's poetry, to lines that represent the liminal appearance of the beloved in the uncertain evidence of sounds
outside.

> Xiaoyu then went and sat by her mother, who said to her,
> "You are always fond of reciting:
>> 'When I opened the curtains, wind stirred the
>> bamboo,
>> and I thought it was my old friend coming.'
> Those lines are from a poem by this very Li Yi. Better to see
> him in person than to spend the whole day imagining him as
> you recite."

In a romantic context, the "old friend" is the beloved. Huo
Xiaoyu's mother's comment on these lines reveals the role of
the discursive culture of romance in the staged encounter.
The image of romance in poetry has *already* captured Huo
Xiaoyu's imagination even before she meets the beloved; she
recites the lines continually, imagining the author; text precedes sex. Yet Xiaoyu's favorite couplet obliquely prefigures
her fate: to spend a long span in just such a state of unful-

filled anticipation, awaiting in vain the return of her old love.

The young couple banter about the meeting of matched "talent" and "beauty." They drink, she sings, and anyone who knows the conventional phase-markers toward intimacy realizes that the bedroom scene must come next.

> The instant she took off her gauze robes, he saw that her body was gorgeous. They lowered the bed curtains and drew close to one another on the pillows, experiencing the transports of pleasure. To Li Yi's mind even what happened on Wu Mountain and by the banks of the Luo could not have been better.

No sooner are the clichés of sexual intercourse described than Huo Xiaoyu begins to weep, and contractual negotiations resume, this time on the duration and firmness of the relationship. Initially, on one level, we had a simple symmetry of plots: boy seeks girl, and girl seeks boy; boy sees girl and desires her; girl desires boy and accepts him; they go to bed. Negotiation is the means by which election is realized and the ceremony of passion staged. Immediately after consummation—indeed Huo Xiaoyu tells us that her anxieties came "at pleasure's height," echoing a song attributed to Emperor Wu of the Han, in which sad thoughts come at the moment of greatest joy—the new question of duration arises, and a new set of negotiations, this time between the principals, begins.

Huo Xiaoyu begins by invoking the social order, the disparity of station between them. Without the support of the conventional social order, he will cast her off as freely as he has chosen her. The earlier set-piece dialogue regarding the balance of "talent" and "beauty" already carries with it the issue of duration; talent is presumed to be lifelong, whereas beauty has a fixed term. When that term is passed, Li Yi will forsake her, but she will not be able to forsake him. When the question of duration arises, the initial narrative of desire, parallel and equal, is exposed as unequal.

Perhaps the most interesting question is why Li Yi cannot

simply say, "Yes, that's true." He cannot, of course, acknowledge that he may well cast her off after a time. That prohibition, however much we take it for granted, is at the center of the code of romance. Before he makes his vow never to abandon her, Li Yi says, "Today I have gained everything that I hoped for in this life." The romantic act of choice cannot be like choosing a grapefruit; it is choosing for oneself absolutely. Although the word has become so devalued by misuse that we forget its radical implications, it is "commitment" of oneself.

Such an act of commitment involves overvaluing. I am using this term in a formal sense and not as a personal judgment. The beloved is invested with unlimited value, far in excess of that person's value as socially constituted or as a sexual object. Like wit, this is the production of surplus value in an exchange system of cultural values. Romance is largely a discourse of valuing, and the valuation is always excessive and frequently measured against other things of large value— one's life, one's social standing, the totality of one's property. These other things of great value are frequently spent to confirm or preserve romantic love.

The discourse between lovers, or between a lover and a member of the larger community, often bears an uncomfortable resemblance to haggling. Many narratives of romance are constructed around events that demonstrate relative valuation. Just as the question of duration discursively resists limits, the act of valuing must go beyond all socially reasonable assessments of value.

Both the witty poet of the garden and the lover produce an interpretive surplus of value. The difference is, of course, that romantic commitment is unironic; it is risking oneself to sustain the act of willful and singular overvaluing. In "Choosing a Dwelling Place in Luoyang" Bai Juyi proclaimed a similar commitment to his Taihu rocks and his pet crane; but he could still go to the office the next day. Bai was also attracted to the discourse of singular commitment, but it was unproblematic because it was pure play. Romantic commitment was the attempt to institute the individual act of valuation in the social world, or, as here, to represent such an act.[7]

This absolute act of choice negates the possibility of narrative. It is the choice to live "happily ever after," outside time. The condition of being in love does not admit development, except in degree. Fictions of romance often refer to (but cannot describe in a temporally differentiated way) a phase of bliss, an unchanging condition of indeterminate duration. Only the disruption of bliss returns us to narrative.

The lover makes the choice not to be compelled by outside forces; that is, his is the self-reflexive form of autonomous choice, the choice to be autonomous. Earlier we discussed the development of a private sphere as the counterpart of the medieval idea of reclusion. I hope it will not seem too strange to suggest that not only is the culture of romance another version of the private sphere, but it is also an even more perfect counterpart of reclusion. In the public world, things change; the world of the recluse and the bliss of lovers are unchanging states of being and require commitment. The amusements of one's garden are merely temporary, but possible; the bliss of lovers is envisioned as something without term, hence its conventional figuration in terms of gods and immortals. Like reclusion, it is predicated on resistance to the social order; but unlike reclusion it incorporates another person, creating the impossible reconciliation of a minimal society and absolute autonomy. It is impossible in any pragmatic sense, but its power as an idea was immense, in traditional China as in many other societies.

To return to "Huo Xiaoyu's Story": this is why Li Yi cannot say, "Yes, I will probably cast you off when you become unlovely or inconvenient." A person who could say that belongs

---

[7] Here it is important to keep in mind that in Tang elite society romantic commitment and the socially sanctioned institution of marriage could not easily be reconciled, as we have attempted to do in the contemporary world. To carry out what he promises, Li Yi would have to stand against family and the larger body of social opinion; it would probably have ruined his career.

in the brothel rather than in the culture of romance in the demimonde. Li Yi answers Huo Xiaoyu's anxiety by writing a generic "lover's oath"; the text gives us no details regarding what he wrote, but observes: "Every line showed the utmost sincerity, and whoever heard it was much moved."

The phrasing here and elsewhere is interesting, suggesting that throughout the relationship between Li Yi and Huo Xiaoyu there is a public world of witnesses, who know the intimacies that pass between the lovers. It is, indeed, that *public* world of witnesses that ultimately enforce the code of romance, criticizing Li Yi for his behavior and ultimately compelling Li Yi to witness Huo Xiaoyu's last moments. The following is Huo Xiaoyu's death scene:

> When she saw Li Yi, she held back her anger and gazed at him fixedly, saying nothing. Her wasted flesh and lovely features gave the impression that she could endure it no longer. For a moment she hid her face behind her sleeve, then looked back at Li Yi. Such things touch people painfully, and everyone present was sobbing. In a little while a few dozen dishes of food and jugs of wine were brought in from the outside. Everyone present was startled to see this, and they immediately asked where the food had come from. All of it had been sent by the bold-hearted gentleman in the yellow shirt. When the food and drink was laid out, they went to sit down.

From the bedroom oath in the beginning to the death scene above, what we would assume to be a supremely private and enclosed relation between the lovers is, in fact, presented as public, its end witnessed over a catered meal. Others often make their presence felt, judging and participating in the story. The public sides with Huo Xiaoyu, and, in their opinions and actions, they support romantic commitment against authorized social demands. Readers are placed in the same position. In this anonymous audience, we have the internal representation of the role of the romantic fiction within society. Members of society cannot live the romantic fiction, but they can demand it. What they cannot choose for themselves, they choose for others. And the term "choose" here is the absolute lover's choice. It is, on reflection, remarkable that for all the claims about the dominance of values of filial duty in traditional China, it is virtually impossible to see Li Yi's behavior in obeying his mother in a positive, Confucian light. The story makes it obvious that there was a code of romance in Tang China whose claims could, in certain narrative conditions, be seen as higher than those of the Confucian social order.

Once Li Yi writes the lover's oath in the bedroom on their first night together, Li Yi and Huo Xiaoyu enter the phase of bliss. As was common in Tang tales, vast spans of bliss pass very quickly: "From then on they clung to one another like kingfishers in the paths through the clouds. They were together day and night like this for two years." Bliss defies narrative and perhaps all discourse.

Passing the examination and the formal entrance of the young man into public life were often important events in Tang tales: they set a "term," a limit to duration in narrative. At this point the relationship either could be regularized or, as was more often the case, become threatened by the larger social world, ready to write its own conventional social plot over the romantic plot. Here at a party given when Li Yi has been selected for office, we have one of the most remarkable moments in "Huo Xiaoyu's Story." Huo Xiaoyu asks for a second oath, this one setting a term of eight years to their relationship, after which Li Yi will be released from his vow and returned to the unromantic public world where he can contract a socially sanctioned marriage. Huo Xiaoyu will herself become a nun. This eminently sensible compromise between the romance narrative and society's conventional plot for a promising young civil servant cannot be permitted to happen.

Our earlier discussion of private spaces is helpful here. Such spaces circumscribe a domain of the private *within* the social world, both separated from it yet contained within it, just as, in the West, the work of art appears within the social world, separated from it by the frame or the edge of the stage. "My" land exists within the emperor's land, yet remains mine; "my" experiences occur within a public life that is subject to the emperor's whim, yet the moment remains mine. Since the poet of the private sphere works on small things and enclosed spaces, he can also accept the temporal limitation of his pleasures: they are explicitly for the "free time from public duties," *gongxia* 公暇. It is to such a possibility of a bounded term of autonomy within a larger world of social determination that Huo Xiaoyu appeals.

And again we must pose the question: Why can't Li Yi accept this? His refusal of Huo Xiaoyu's proposal is a radicalized version of the poet's "Don't tell me X," in which X is some commonsense view of the poet's interpretive extravagance. Here we might recall the treason of the medieval recluse in Kong Zhigui's "North Mountain Proclamation." Like the recluse, Li Yi has made an absolute choice, an unchanging condition and not a move within a narrative. Any backing away from that commitment is betrayal of the rejection of limits that lies at the heart of romance. But Li Yi has passed the examination and is embarking on a political career, which is society's narrative for him. Although he cannot relax his grip on it, his romantic commitment is already an illusion. Asked by Huo Xiaoyu to accept limitation, he must refuse, however disastrous the consequences.

Facing one woman, Huo Xiaoyu, Li Yi must reaffirm his absolute commitment to romance. Facing another woman, his mother, he must commit himself to the narrative that pleases her. Just as he cannot break role as "the lover" to the first woman, he cannot break role as "the dutiful son" to the other. This is the tragedy of the man incapable of irony. The narrative of "the lover" and the narrative of "the dutiful son" cannot be reconciled (except by the ironist), and for this reason Li Yi cannot bring himself to face Huo Xiaoyu again. In her presence he will have to be "the lover" again. And, indeed, when he is dragged to face her death scene and when he meets her after her death, he responds with apparent sincerity as the lover.

Always underneath the story is the question of who supports the relationship, who pays. There is a disturbing symmetry here. While Li Yi is out gathering money for the bride-price of the woman his mother has chosen, Huo Xiaoyu is spending her fortune to get word of Li Yi. Huo Xiaoyu's expenditures are the counterpart of those of the infatuated young man who uses up his fortune for the sake of the beloved; like the infatuated young man, she receives the sympathy and support of those who understand the world of romance in the demimonde. Expenditure is, it seems, the proof of valuing. For Li Yi the extravagant bride-price is a mark of social value, the cost of marrying into a distinguished family. But Huo Xiaoyu's expenditure is a private assignment of value, and in spending everything she has, she points to a value that transcends the estimation of worth commonly agreed upon by society. Her audience approves; if they themselves cannot produce a private system of value, they honor the possibility. Bai Juyi pretends a similar system of values with his Taihu rocks and his crane; he succeeds because nothing is really at stake. Huo Xiaoyu risks, loses, and wins esteem.

The question of Huo Xiaoyu's own "value" is inseparable from her ambiguous social status. In speaking her anxieties to Li Yi on their first night together, she states her status in no uncertain terms: "I come from a courtesan background," *qie ben changjia* 妾本倡家. But she is also the daughter of a Tang prince, removed from the family after the prince's death because she inherits her mother's status as a professional performer; at the same time she is acknowledged by the family in being given a share of the family property. Xiaoyu is herself the fruit of romance, and she well understands that such a relationship cannot have the duration that comes only through social sanction. Unable to enter into a socially sanctioned relationship and unwilling to be the entertainer that she proclaims as her lineage, Huo Xiaoyu uses the "value" inherited from her father to act autonomously; she freely disposes of her body and her wealth, recognizing that both have a limited term. But Li Yi traps her by refusing to agree on the term.

In one of the most famous incidents in the story, in which values of many different kinds come together, Huo Xiaoyu at last pawns a hairpin of purple jade that had been the gift of her father, the Prince of Huo. Her maidservant takes it to the marketplace where it is recognized by an old jade carver, the very man who had long ago fashioned it as a gift from the prince to his daughter. He elicits the story from the maid, and greatly moved, he takes her to the household of a Tang princess where the story is told "in detail." The princess is also moved and gives the maid money to take back to Huo Xiaoyu. This is a fine intersection between the individual act of overvaluing (spending all she has for word of her lover who has obviously proved faithless) and the broader circle of those who are interested in romance and share its values. Huo Xiaoyu's story begins to be told and retold as a story within the narrative—it circulates. The princess is touched by the story and pays, like a member of the audience, so that the story can continue.

"By silence and having her hear nothing from him, he wanted to put an end to Xiaoyu's hopes." Li Yi's silence, his careful evasions, and his inability to face Huo Xiaoyu are among the most striking moments in the story. No less remarkable is Huo Xiaoyu's entrapment by Li Yi's uncompleted word, despite all the evidence that he has forsaken her and even on hearing of his betrayal from others. For Huo Xiaoyu, in order for there to be an ending Li Yi must return and speak, or be spoken to. Unable to reconcile the absolute lover with the dutiful son, Li Yi seeks to simply erase Huo Xiaoyu from his life, only to find that it is not possible. Even out of sight, Huo Xiaoyu is always present as a fixed place to be avoided. If he goes out with his friends, they sympathize with her and criticize him. Unable to accept the limited private space of the garden, the limitation of duration, or the irony that permits one to be both engaged and distant, Li Yi had attempted to institute a relationship without limiting boundaries and thus a relationship that would be continuous with social life. He instituted it by words, by "giving his word." And now, unless he stands before Huo Xiaoyu and takes back his word, his creation will not go away. And he is still incapable of the necessary retraction.

Huo Xiaoyu had proposed her own version of the story. Li Yi refused it and insisted on his own version. She accepted his version, and now she cannot get out of his version of the story until he shows himself and changes his word. All this becomes publicly known. He told her: I will love you forever, wait for me, I will send for you. That story is on hold. Now he tells new stories to others, but he still cannot end the first story; he cannot just leave it hanging. The audience grows restless and begins to intrude into the story—by conveying information, passing judgments on the protagonists, and eventually intervening to bring the story to a conclusion. Li Yi has lost control of his story.

Finally the man in the yellow shirt intervenes. He does so by lying, by telling Li Yi of the pleasures he will enjoy if he comes along with him. And Li Yi finds himself coerced back into the story he started long before, the story he left incomplete. His presence makes an ending possible, and he is the necessary witness of Huo Xiaoyu's death scene. Now it is Huo Xiaoyu's turn to tell a story, that of how it will be for the rest of Li Yi's life; she will become a vengeful ghost. Huo Xiaoyu does not leave her story incomplete.

We might note the particular nature of the revenge of Huo Xiaoyu's spirit. Supernatural intervention is necessary only in the beginning—the shadow of a man by the bedcurtain, tokens tossed in a window. The "ghost," if there is one, seems to know how to spark something that is already present in Li Yi's nature and history. Nothing else needs to be done. Li Yi comes to distrust the fidelity of his wives and concubines; he casts them out, kills them, or terrorizes them. The question always turns on his ability to exert control over their feelings and desires, a social control hopelessly set against their autonomy. The power to freely choose whom one loves, which is the very basis of romance, becomes Li Yi's nightmare. Just as he chose to accept social compulsion for himself, he attempts to coerce others, frantic because he knows that he cannot control feeling. All this darkly echoes the opening, in which Li Yi, anxious and uncertain, receives Huo Xiaoyu's love and faith by *her* free choice, a choice unencumbered by financial necessity. All the subsequent women in his life live in *his* house; he supports them; he has bought them. And in this case the autonomy of choice, essential to romance and fidelity, becomes uncertain and threatening. If the woman were free to choose, she might choose someone else. In this way Li Yi is haunted and destroyed.

Conflicting Interpretations: "Yingying's Story"

"Yingying's Story" 鶯鶯傳 by Yuan Zhen 元稹 (779–831) is undoubtedly the most problematic narrative of the Tang. Its vernacular transformation into the fourteenth-century variety play *An Account of the Western Porch, Xixiang ji* 西廂記, gave the story a happy ending and tried to resolve the troublesome issues it raised. But even the insistently moralizing commentary on the play by the famous seventeenth-century critic Jin Shengtan 金聖歎 could not entirely get the story under control.

Our interests here are not to decide whether the tale is or is not an autobiographical account of an affair of Yuan Zhen. This can never be known with historical certainty. By looking closely at the story we can, however, say that *if* the story were autobiographical, the author would have done something very strange in figuring himself as the protagonist Zhang. If the story were autobiographical, Yuan Zhen would either be displaying a rare capacity to represent the complexity of a relationship, with the rights and wrongs involved, or would be engaging in a wondrously blind attempt at self-exculpation, an attempt that forcefully undermines the case he is trying to make.

"Yingying's Story" is unique among Tang tales in sustaining two opposing points of view, each of which tries to take control of the story and compel judgment in its favor. The interpretation of events and the judgment that follows from

such interpretation is the prize at stake. Our ability to pass
sure moral judgment finally fails, but that failure does not
mean that the account is indifferent to the moral judgments
readers might render; the story begs us to pass judgment. In
the end, the disputants are deadlocked, and each has so
thoroughly discredited the other that we are left with no secure ground to decide between them. On the one side is the
venerable cultural image of the femme fatale, ingratiating and
manipulative, feigning huffs and passions to gain her will. On
the other side are the values of the culture of romance, values
that can be seen in "Huo Xiaoyu's Story." In a freely contracted romantic liaison, the public honor of both parties is at
stake; lovers are supposed to maintain their commitment,
and the man's betrayal can earn him the lasting opprobrium
of the community. "Yingying's Story" still possesses the remarkable capacity to call forth the intense allegiances of
readers to one side or another of this ancient argument between the sexes. Let us take sides if we must (allowing that
women often support Zhang against Yingying and men often
support Yingying against Zhang), but we should keep in mind
that when this story was written, *both* sets of values were in
existence and both claims were powerful.

The contending viewpoints of "Yingying's Story" appear in
the context of discursive conflicts of interpretation in the Mid-
Tang. On a trivial level Bai Juyi, the witty poet of the garden,
maintains his overblown interpretations against the commonsense perspective that he himself introduces and sustains.
More than any writer in centuries, Han Yu is polemical, argu-
ing against positions he constructs. Meng Jiao repeatedly
disputes sweet commonplaces with a rhetorical "Who claims"
shei wei 誰謂. Liu Zongyuan cheerfully offers several explanations for the presence of Little Stone Ramparts Mountain in
the wilderness around Yongzhou, only to dismiss them all.
But more seems to be at stake in making a judgment in
"Yingying's Story," and the conflict of interpretations is not so
easily controlled. It may not have been intentional, but literary history attests how frequently the problems set in play in

an age can overwhelm the author's most dedicated attempts to offer a simple resolution.

The story begins as it ends, with young Zhang trying to justify his behavior to his friends.[1] This frame constructs an internal audience for the story, an audience that by the end is given an account of Zhang's affair with Yingying and is called upon to pass judgment.

In the Zhenyuan Reign [785-804] there was a certain man named Zhang, of a gentle nature and handsome appearance. He held steadfastly to his personal principles and refused to become involved in anything improper. Sometimes a group of friends would go off to a party and behave riotously. While the others tried to outdo one another in wanton and unbridled recklessness, Zhang would remain utterly composed, and they could never get him to act in an intemperate manner. At this time he was twenty-three and had never been intimate with a woman. When a close friend questioned him about this, Zhang excused himself say, "The famous lecher of antiquity, Deng Tuzi, was not a man of passionate desire; his were the actions of a brute. I am someone who has authentic passionate desire, but simply have not encountered it. How can I say this? Creatures of the most bewitching beauty never fail to leave a lasting impression on my heart, and this tells me that I am not one of those free of passion." And the one who had questioned him acknowledged this in him.

One reading to which we are directed by the exemplary anecdote in the beginning and the closing judgment is a story of moral "development." Through a slight fall from grace and subsequent repentance, a young man grows up and learns from his mistakes. To tell such a story we could begin with his blind claim in this opening passage about his susceptibility to "creatures of the most bewitching beauty," *wu zhi youzhe* 物之尤者, and measure this against his later realization of the dangers of "creatures of bewitching beauty," *youwu* 尤物,

---

[1] For a translation of "Yingying's Story," see pp. 192–204.

with the full weight of Confucian fear of male disempower-
ment behind that ancient term.

There is indeed a voice in the text that tries to offer such
an odious reading, but that voice fails to control the narrative. Yingying is too engrossing and sometimes too vulnerable
to be reduced to the mere narrative instrument of Zhang's
moral education. We might attempt to redeem such a reading
by suggesting that unlike lesser fictions, in which *youwu* are
sketched only on the surface and from the distance, here we
are to be given an adequate representation of *youwu*, revealing the compelling force of personality that makes them so
engrossing and thus so dangerous. But insofar as the representation of *youwu* is adequate in that way, we can no longer
glibly "learn a lesson" from it; it can attract us and take command of the text. As with Milton's Satan, if we attempt to
sustain the reading that supports public morality, we are
forced to confront the true power of the dangerous alternative
and discover a strong party in ourselves that would make the
choice against public morality.

The reading of the story that makes it a lesson in Confucian moral development is destabilized by a too perfect representation of the occasion and the force of private desire. An
alternative reading is no less implicit in the story. This reading comes from the contemporary culture of romance, whose
values are embodied in "Huo Xiaoyu's Story." Like the inter-
fering audience in "Huo Xiaoyu's Story," Zhang's friends seem
inclined to this interpretation. In this version of the story, the
young man encounters a young woman who is capable of
both passion and devotion, who gives herself to him of her
own free will. Such a relationship is valued because it is
based on feeling rather than social obligation. The young
man, however, is unable to appreciate such purity of commitment. Driven by self-serving motives of his own political
career, he casually abandons her and puts her from his
mind.

Unfortunately this reading is undermined as thoroughly
as the Confucian moralizing reading. The theatricality of

Yingying's passion is hard to ignore. Yingying is a young woman performing an image of romantic passion and intensely self-conscious about how she appears. Unlike Huo Xiaoyu, Yingying *can* become a legitimate wife, and she is well aware of this. The suspicion of a social motive makes the purity of her passionate commitment suspect. The subversion of the romantic ideal is completed toward the end of the story when, after swearing faithfulness until death, she marries (less advantageously) a year after Zhang abandons her.

In this story we have a conflict between two social codes of value, each of which tries to shape the interpretation of the narrative in its own way. Each, however, successfully undermines the other to such a degree that we are left with a story that is credibly human rather than exemplary and governed by a single code of values. Modern readers will still argue passionately for one or the other interpretation. That is, in itself, significant. Dispute is inconceivable about the values behind "Huo Xiaoyu's Story" or virtually any other Tang tale. "Yingying's Story" is the fruit of the Mid-Tang, a world where values and meaning have become destabilized.

The process of destabilization begins early in the story. In the passage quoted above, we seem to be presented with a simple opposition between virtue and licentiousness. This is the paradigm in "The Poetic Exposition on Deng Tuzi's Lust" 登徒子好色賦 alluded to in the passage. In that work Deng Tuzi accuses the rhetorician Song Yu of "lust" or "passionate desire," *haose* 好色. Song Yu responds that he is free of lust because his eastern neighbor, one of the most beautiful women in the world, has been eyeing him for three years, and he has not succumbed to her charms. Next Song Yu points out that Deng Tuzi is so attracted to his ugly wife that he has begotten five children; Song Yu concludes by asking which of the two of them is driven by lust. In his self-justification to his friend, Zhang offers a problematic third term: he claims to be "someone who is truly capable of passionate desire" or "authentic lust," *zhen haosezhe* 眞好色者. This "authentic lust" is reserved for "creatures of the most bewitching beauty." Zhang fatefully places himself in the position of a Song Yu who welcomes the advances of the beautiful neighbor, and in doing so injects the code of romance (in which the "young talent," *caizi* 才子, is *supposed* to form a liaison with a "fair maid," *jiaren* 佳人) into the moralist's simple opposition between debauchery and self-restraint.

By the code of romance the "young talent" may be supposed to bed the "fair maid," but the fair maid is never his cousin. When Zhang meets Madame Zheng, he discovers consanguinity on the maternal side (the text is quite explicit about discovering the family connection, removing any possibility that this kinship is a polite fiction).[2] Not only does this provide legitimate grounds for his contact with Madame Zheng and her children, the fact that Yingying is a maternal cousin with a different surname raises the distinct possibility of legitimate marriage.

Zhang arranges for the family's protection during the mutiny of the local garrison, and to thank him Madame Zheng holds a banquet at which her children are to pay their respects to Zhang as their elder brother. If we are inclined to read the text as the author's attempt to exculpate his own behavior, we can see this whole section as justifying his introduction into the family and his meeting with Cui Yingying. Nubile young women of gentry clans were kept from the sight of young men lest flaming passion be aroused on either or both sides. Zhang finds himself in the ambiguous position of elder brother (who is permitted to behold his "sister") and potential suitor. No hint is given of Madame Zheng's motives in arranging this problematic banquet, but it is obvious that Cui Yingying regards the meeting as potentially erotic and hence improper:

> Next [Madame Zheng] gave the order to her daughter: "Come out and pay your respects to your elder brother; you are alive because of him." A long time passed, and then she de-

---

[2] Yingying's mother is sometimes referred to by her maiden name Zheng, and sometimes by her married name Cui.

clined on the excuse that she wasn't feeling well. Madame Cui said angrily, "Mr. Zhang protected your life. Otherwise you would have been taken captive. How can you still keep such a wary distance from him!" After another long wait, the daughter came in. She wore everyday clothes and had a disheveled appearance, not having dressed up specially for the occasion. Tresses from the coils of her hair hung down to her eyebrows and her two cheeks were suffused with rosy color. Her complexion was rare and alluring, with a glow that stirred a man. Zhang was startled as she paid him the proper courtesies. Then she sat down beside her mother. Since her mother had forced her to meet Zhang, she stared fixedly away in intense resentment, as if she couldn't bear it. When he asked her age, Madame Cui said, "From September 784, the first year of the emperor's reign, until the present year, 800, makes her seventeen years old." Zhang tried to draw her into conversation, but she wouldn't answer him.

In the opening anecdote Zhang is given the opportunity to explain the motives behind his own behavior. Yingying's unusual behavior, on the other hand, begs for explanation, yet none is offered. There are many things that were certainly true in the Tang world, but were usually excluded from representation. Among these are family tensions, such as the hostilities that can arise between a mother and a teenage daughter. Their inclusion here is a means to point to something going on beneath the surface.

The modern reader (and perhaps even the Tang reader) would be quick to understand this as Yingying's resistance to being put on erotic display before a potential suitor. The modern reader will see this as a sign either of her resistance to her mother's authority or of the intensity of her awareness that Zhang is a potential mate. The naive attempt to make herself unattractive by dishevelment has, of course, quite the opposite effect. And her pout makes her all the more alluring.

The Confucian moralizing interpretation that would make Yingying a *youwu*, a "bewitching creature," would see here the warning signs of her refractory, willful nature and her unpredictability. The code of romance would see much the same thing but interpret these qualities in a more positive light: the scene would demonstrate her passionate nature and resistance to convention.

However we interpret and judge Cui Yingying's behavior, the result is inevitable: Zhang is "infatuated," *huo* 惑, a term that strongly suggests going astray. Although this has strongly negative implications for the moralist, it is precisely such an overwhelming passion that young men go seeking in the world of romance and indeed the kind of passion that Zhang claimed he sought in the opening anecdote.

This is one of the ethical crises of the story, a point where we realize that two socially distinct courtship narratives have become confused. In the narrative that does not occur, Zhang goes to Yingying's mother and arranges to marry Yingying; Hongniang, the maid, and later Yingying herself keep reminding Zhang of this possibility. The second narrative belongs to the code of romance; here passionate love ignores social convention and finds its own way. When reading Zhang's Confucian pieties at the end, we should never forget that at this point Zhang knowingly chooses the romance narrative, and he chooses it in a social context where it loses even its liminal social acceptability—within his own family. What makes "Yingying's Story" almost unique among Tang tales is the way in which the romance narrative slips into domestic, socially legitimate space. This confusion is embodied in the sites of their sexual encounters, sometimes in her quarters and sometimes in his. His knowledge of "the kinship ties of the Cuis," *Cui zhi yinzu* 崔之姻族, of which Hongniang reminds him, is precisely the kind of information that is exchanged in negotiating a proper marriage.

Zhang's objections to Hongniang's suggestion of marriage focuses on the issue of delay. In a proper marriage ritual, delay is the guarantee against the immediacy of passion and the threat that passion poses to the stability of the institution. The duration of engagement is counterpoised against the problem of duration that arises in freely contracted liaisons. From the side of the code of romance, the impatience of passion is the guarantee of genuine feeling. To exist, romance depends upon the display of inner compulsion. Yet the fires of Zhang's compulsion are doused with remarkable ease, first by Hongniang's flight and later by Yingying's rebuff.

Just as she suggested a formal engagement, Hongniang's advice to Zhang on how to win Yingying refuses the image of perfect romance that Zhang evoked in the opening anecdote, the fulfillment of his "authentic lust." In Hongniang's formulation there are none of the ceremonious euphemisms often used in negotiating love affairs in the demimonde. Hongniang is discussing the seduction of a virgin of a good family. Using the term *luan* 亂 for "seducing" Yingying, Hongniang creates an explicit analogy between Zhang's proposed actions and the military disorders (also *luan*) that brought him into first contact with Yingying. A fundamental moral transgression on the part of the male is implied here, and Zhang does not object to the terms used. The moralist's simple story of a weak but good young man besotted by a *youwu* is out of place here.

Huo Xiaoyu was attracted to Li Yi's verses, and Hongniang suggests that Zhang rely on a similar ploy and try to seduce Yingying with poetry. Perhaps the strongest evidence that "Yingying's Story" is meant to exculpate Yuan Zhen under the guise of Zhang is the omission of Zhang's verses and his letter to Yingying, and the inclusion of her own poem and letter. Her verse, in fact, contains a variation on the lines attributed to Li Yi that so attracted Huo Xiaoyu. On receiving her poem, Zhang "understood the subtle message implied," *wei yu qi zhi* 微喻其旨. Although the message turns out to be a most problematic communication, Yingying conveyed her message by representing herself in the future, in a scene of romance. Here we have the first hint that Zhang is not alone in projecting a romance narrative. It is all a question of which of the prospective lovers gets to tell the story.

In the upbraiding scene we have the first violent conflict of discourses. The conventional romance narrative, shading darkly into a seduction story, is exploded by the sudden appearance of Cui Yingying as the "virtuous woman," delivering

a Confucian moral lesson that is supposed to make the of-
fender hang his head with shame.

"By your kindness you saved our family, and that was indeed generous. For this reason my sweet mother entrusted
you with the care of her young son and daughter. But how
could you use this wicked maid to deliver such wanton
verses to me! I first understood your saving us from molestation as virtue, but now you have taken advantage of that to
make your own demands. How much difference is there between one form of molestation and the other? I had truly
wanted to simply ignore your verses, but it would not have
been right to condone such lechery in a person. I would have
revealed them to my mother, but it would have been unlucky
to so turn one's back on a person's kindness. I was going to
have my maid give you a message, but I was afraid she
would not correctly convey how I truly feel. Then I planned to
use a short letter to set this out before you, but I was afraid
you would take it ill. So I used those frivolous and coy verses
to make you come here. Can you avoid feeling shame at
such improper actions? I want most of all that you conduct
yourself properly and not sink to the point where you molest
people!"

It is difficult not to notice that most of Yingying's eloquent
denunciation is spent in justifying her having sent Zhang the
poem with its erotic invitation. The high moral tone that Yingying assumes carried immense authority, but, as so often
happens in Mid-Tang writing, an intuition of circumstantial
motives undermines the authority of discourse. Here, even
more radically than in many other texts we have seen, we are
compelled to an ironic reading of a kind of discourse that was
never supposed to be read ironically. It is not mere common
sense that requires us to question Yingying's motives in her
self-justifying denunciation of Zhang. Yingying herself tells
that she has used one kind of discourse, an erotic "spring
verse," for ulterior motives; she creates the gap between apparent and concealed intentions that invites us to question
her motives now. Our suspicions are confirmed by her subsequent visit to Zhang's bedroom. Clearly the role that she as-

sumes in her denunciation does not transparently or adequately represent her true feelings and intentions.

A large space is opened here for interpretation. We can say that Yingying is an adolescent girl, caught between conflicting impulses; she sent off her "spring verse," then felt ashamed and tried to conceal her original impulse by this elaborate explanation. We can say that Yingying is a *youwu*, whose variability is part of her attraction. We can say that Yingying is the romantic heroine, drawn to virtue as much as to passion, and at last overwhelmed by passion. But whatever interpretation we make, discourse no longer directly represents the feelings, motives, and intentions of the human subject.

Once initiated, such destabilization of the authority of discourse is infectious. Just as we immediately reduce the moral authority of Yingying's self-justification to her motives, so we cannot help doing the same to the moral authority of Zhang's equally self-justifying speech to his friends later in the story. The author may not have "intended" that we do so, but he has himself introduced hermeneutic forces into the story that cannot be controlled. Now that we think about it, we had similar suspicions in the beginning when Zhang justifies his behavior at parties to his friend; we also suspected that Madame Zheng arranged the banquet so that Zhang would be attracted to Yingying (already seventeen and not yet engaged) and ask for her hand in marriage. Here with Yingying's "virtuous woman" speech and later with Zhang's discourse of wise restraint in avoiding a *youwu*, we have statements of shared moral values that have lost much of their power to compel assent because they have been deployed for purely personal motives.

The scenes in which Zhang confesses his passion to Hongniang have a remarkable homology with the paired encounters with Yingying herself. The male makes the first, transgressive move; he is reproached by the woman and withdraws in shame; then the woman takes the initiative. There is even a trace of this pattern in the apparently gratuitous parrot scene in "Huo Xiaoyu's Story."

Denounced, Zhang loses hope and even seems to accept the situation. Then one night Hongniang comes into the room using exactly the same words she had used when Zhang crept into the girls' apartments: "She's here! She's here!" It is as if the upbraiding scene were some strange aberration, and the present scene were picking up the narrative thread of romance where it had left off. In fact, the romantic narrative has been significantly changed; there is a new storyteller—Yingying herself. Unlike the problematic seduction (*luan*) narrative that Zhang was trying to write, Yingying is writing a more ancient romance in which the woman controls the encounter. Yingying is playing the goddess of Wu Mountain, who visits the king of Chu in a dream and then departs at her pleasure: "he wondered if she might not be one of those goddesses or fairy princesses, for he could not believe that she came from this mortal world." Yingying is perhaps no less drawn to a romance narrative than Zhang, but she wants to revise the script so that she is the protagonist rather than the victim. And, of course, this can be taken as yet another piece of evidence that she is a *youwu*.

Yingying is, unfortunately, not a goddess. She is an adolescent girl of a respectable, if not notable, family. Although she may be drawn to the romance narrative, her virginity is an important commodity in that more pedestrian story of a socially acceptable marriage. She may have been able to talk her way out of having sent Zhang the "spring verse," but in deciding to play the goddess, Yingying has made a fatal error. She has now become dependent on Zhang's continuing affection, and because of the disparity in power that such dependency creates, her subsequent attempts to assert control over the situation can only appear as "manipulation." And it must be said that she has already created the space for interpreting her words and deeds as manipulation by her own behavior and explanation of her "spring verse."

Far more than Zhang, Yingying has a flair for the theatrical, for playing a role within a scene. The sheer variety of roles she plays and their excess contribute to our inability to find a stable Yingying behind her appearances. She has played the pouting daughter, the exemplary woman of virtue, and the mysterious goddess. In her letter to Zhang she will assume the role of the self-effacing wife, and in the second half of the story she will play many variations on the woman cruelly abandoned. Although Zhang himself is (perhaps unwittingly) represented to us as someone without any redeeming qualities, there may be some justification in one of the charges he levels against Yingying at the end: he speaks of her "transformations," *bianhua* 變化, and the sense of threat such transformations can create. Her unpredictability frightens him.

At first, however, Zhang is the willing participant in Yingying's mythic sexual theater. After her departure on the first night, he wonders if it was all a dream, then finds verification in the lingering traces of her presence. Then in a few days, once the liquids evaporate and the scent fades, he is no longer certain. At this point the entire liminal experience is represented in his incomplete poem "Meeting the Holy One" 會眞詩.

There is a reciprocal relation in "Yingying's Story" between events and their various representations—in poems, letters, explanations, and even in projective images whose presence we infer by the way in which events occur. In her "spring verse," Yingying romantically imagines a scene in which the stirring shadows of flowers make her wonder if her lover is coming; we may legitimately suspect that her visit to Zhang also enacts a romantic image she formed before the event. By writing "Meeting the Holy One," Zhang accepts and participates in the images of Yingying's version of the romance narrative (very different from the seduction story Zhang originally anticipated). Only upon receiving the poem that confirms his participation in her story will Yingying bed him again.

There remains, however, a serious problem. The poem is

uncompleted and must be left incomplete. In the story of the goddess of Wu Mountain and in the derivative legends of immortal women choosing mortal lovers, the mortal man is at last forsaken and left in hopeless longing. At this stage of their relationship Zhang is obviously not going to encourage such a conclusion, and although such an ending might appeal to Yingying's images of her own empowerment, it conflicts with the imperatives of the social situation, which demand that she marry Zhang.

Yingying's mother, who may have initially wanted to put Yingying on display in order to whet Zhang's appetite for a marriage proposal, now finds herself with a disaster. A brief and ambiguous passage glosses over immense problems, leaving us certain only that Yingying or her mother wants Zhang to "regularize the situation." This is one of those moments when we see the power of narrative silence. Immediately following the suggestion on the part of Yingying or her mother that Zhang marry Yingying properly, the text announces Zhang's departure for Chang'an, for unstated reasons, and his return several months later. The inclusion of the request that Zhang formally marry Yingying (with the already established consanguinity that makes such a marriage acceptable) lets us know that marriage *is* an issue. The narrative silence in response strongly suggests that Zhang has no intention of doing so. Moreover, the story's representation of Zhang's ability to come and go as he pleases forcefully demonstrates that he now has control of the story. In other words, the goddess may come in the middle of the night and let the man enjoy her favors, but we are in a different kind of story altogether when the man leaves on a business trip and returns at his convenience.

> Not long afterward Zhang was to go off to Chang'an, and before he went he consoled her by telling her of his love. Yingying seemed to raise no complaints, but the sad expression of reproach on her face was very moving. Two evenings before he was to travel, she refused to see him again.
>
> Zhang subsequently went west to Chang'an. After several

months he again visited Puzhou, and this time his meetings with Yingying lasted a series of months.

Yingying's refusal to see Zhang before his departure is Yingying's last valiant attempt to recapture her version of the story, in which she is the goddess and Zhang, the suppliant lover. Her only power is to come when she chooses and be absent when she chooses. Zhang demonstrates that he can do the same. The line that follows, "Zhang subsequently went west to Chang'an," again shows the force of narrative silence and Yingying's complete loss of control over the situation. The narrative includes her refusal to see Zhang; it says nothing of Zhang's response, only that he left. Although the narrative will tell us later that he was infatuated with her, his romantic pleasure is now to be conducted on his terms and according to his timetable: "after several months he again visited Puzhou." In "Huo Xiaoyu's Story" Li Yi was helpless and so trapped between conflicting claims that he could not face Huo Xiaoyu; Zhang, in contrast, is perfectly willing to bed Yingying and play the game of romance when it is convenient.

Zhang's second visit to Puzhou focuses on Yingying's literary and musical skills, both of which she withholds from Zhang. This withholding creates a private space to which Zhang is denied access, now that he has access to her body at his pleasure. Whether we interpret this as a strategy to recreate the conditions of male desire or simply a human attempt to reestablish an identity that is not at Zhang's mercy, the effect is predictably the same: "with this Zhang became even more infatuated with her." Although Zhang later will describe Yingying as a *youwu* and express his fears for the consequences that would have followed if he had remained with her, it is clear that this is exactly what Zhang wants Yingying to be. He loses interest because she shows her dependency and vulnerability in trying to hold him by guilt. A true *youwu* would bind Zhang absolutely; Yingying only plays at being a *youwu*, just as she plays at being the goddess.

Zhang's infatuations are, however, pleasurable experiences of no significant duration. Immediately after announcing this resurgence of infatuation, the narrator announces that Zhang has to go off to Chang'an to take the examination. On this occasion Zhang does not inform Yingying of his departure; rather, Yingying divines it as he sighs "sadly" by her side. This is an interesting moment, when we have the first intimation of guilt on Zhang's part, guilt that will eventually fuel his attempts at self-justification. When Zhang takes the power to guide the story away from Yingying, guilt replaces desire.

Yingying is aware of Zhang's guilt and plays on it. With a "calm voice" she tells him that his betrayal was quite proper; then she claims to be worried about his melancholy and offers to play the zither to cheer him up. This is followed by the wonderful zither scene in which she breaks down in the middle of her performance and flees the stage. This music scene is the stylized representation of genuine feeling as that which lies behind and breaks through a surface of control. But how are we to read Yingying's "consoling" interpretation of Zhang's behavior that precedes it.

> "It is quite proper that when a man seduces a woman, he finally abandons her. I don't dare protest. It was inevitable that having seduced me, you would end it—all this is by your grace. And with this our lifelong vows are indeed ended. Why be deeply troubled by this journey?"

What are we to make of this transparent fiction of Yingying's feelings, a fiction that we know Zhang can see through as well as ourselves? It is yet another example of Yingying's playing a role, although in this case a role that she does not intend to be believed. As with the "spring verse," Yingying creates gaps and inversions between appearances and true intentions. If this is the case, is the breakdown in her performance any less theatrical?

At this moment we must recall that this is a male narrative. Yuan Zhen, the author, may well be the Zhang of the story, and even if he is not, insofar as the story is based on actual events, Zhang's account is the source of what gets told. Thus the representation of Yingying is motivated, even as Yingying's self-representation is motivated. Nothing can be trusted in this story; the authority of every representation is undermined by unstated motives. The narrator so often illustrates the existence of unexpressed desires behind Yingying's behavior and words that he teaches the reader a mode of interpretation that infects the larger narrative. And yet if every surface is "false," *jia* 假, in the sense that it is shaped by hidden motives, this form of representation keeps leading us back to a ground of all falseness in true feeling and the "genuine," *zhen* 眞: Yingying's motive, her desire to hold Zhang's love, is clearly genuine, as is the narrator's desire to exculpate Zhang's behavior in some way. In neither case is such a ground in the genuine feeling of self-interest enough to entirely redeem the characters.

These issues of representation and motive are forcefully demonstrated in the section on the letter. Yingying's letter is a beautiful example of Tang eloquence, in which feeling, rhetoric, and gracious deference are held in a delicate balance. We can read the letter as an innocent expression of Yingying's feelings; we can read the letter as a manipulative attempt to bind him by guilt. But we should have learned by now to look to the narrator's motives as well as to Yingying's motives. We learn to notice omissions; for example, that Zhang's letter to Yingying is not included. Much in Yingying's letter is clearly a direct response to what he wrote; but without the inclusion of his letter, we read what she writes very differently. With a little effort we can reconstruct what he said, by reading her response.

Zhang wrote "to set her mind to rest," *yi guang qi yi* 以廣其意, ignoring that his letter to her must have declared his feelings for her, no less than her letter declares feelings for him. He sent her gifts, the kind of gifts that would be appropriate only from a man to his beloved; her gifts are only answers to his. What is presented in the story as her one-sided passion bears telltale traces of a mutual exchange. Something has been suppressed here—imperfectly suppressed. We can ignore the traces of the narrator's motives no more than we can ignore the evidence of Yingying's motives.

Why does the narrator introduce it by saying that the letter is "roughly recorded here," *cu zai yu ci* 粗載於此? "Roughly," *cu* 粗, suggests that the present text is somehow imperfect, reconstructed, or incomplete. The text of the letter is anything but "rough"; it is no summary, but a fully developed love letter, the sort one might expect a wife to write to a husband. To what degree is this the admission that this text, from which we would read so much of Yingying's motives and personality, is a re-creation?

Throughout "Yingying's Story" we see the gap between cultural roles and genuine feeling. The narrative generates what we also find in other Mid-Tang writing: the powerful but hazy presence of "real people" who are distinct from the roles they play—who may deploy those roles, be trapped by those roles, resist those roles. We do not know how human beings really "are" in the world, but we can observe how they are represented. These "real people" are supposed to be primary, and the roles or images they inhabit are supposed to be secondary. But on the level of representation itself, "real people" are the secondary phenomenon, produced by slippages in cultural roles and images, produced by ironizing those roles and images or making them a function of motives that have been displaced elsewhere. The disjunction between the formality of Yingying's letter and its urgency seems to perfectly embody this process. The various roles it assumes and the strategies it employs direct readers to the motives of a "someone" behind the text. The letter makes Zhang feel guilty, it wheedles him, and finally it assumes the pose of the concerned wife, worrying that he will catch cold and urging him to circumspection. The "someone" thus produced is indefinite and open to interpretation: she may be a desperate young woman, torn between anger and love; she may be instinctively manipulative; she may be the dangerous *youwu*, whose transformations are beyond comprehension. But whoever she is, she is not transparently identical to what she says.

She tells him, "Be careful of what you say and guard yourself," *shenyan zibao* 慎言自保. The epistolary politeness becomes literal. Immediately afterward we are told that Zhang showed the letter to his friends and the affair became widely known. This is either a willful and brilliant irony or the supreme example of narratorial blindness in world literature. Keeping "Huo Xiaoyu's Story" in mind, we note that Zhang has, like Li Yi, contracted a love affair and then betrayed his beloved. In addition, Zhang is involved with someone he could legitimately marry as first wife, and there is no indication that he has been betrothed elsewhere. Divulging the affair opens Zhang to precisely the kind of criticism that Li Yi had to bear. In the poetic responses of Zhang's friends there are strong hints of such public sympathy for Yingying—although the narrator goes to great pains to assert that, with a full explanation, public opinion came around to Zhang's side.

This phase of the story leads us to wonder about the boundary between the public and the personal in the Tang. Here we might recall how the narrative opened, with Zhang's friends engaging in orgies from which Zhang abstained (at parties with singing girls in the Tang, sex could be at least semipublic, with couples wandering off into the bushes together). Zhang was questioned about his earlier behavior, and in showing the letter and divulging his liaison with Yingying, Zhang validates his claim and demonstrates his heterosexual masculinity to his friends. The affair is "remarkable," and on divulging it, Zhang releases the story into a world of representations—the world of gossip, poetry, prose retelling, and evaluative discussion underlying many Mid-Tang tales. Zhang seems, however, not quite to understand the difference between hiring sex at a party and debauching his maternal cousin. Nor is he troubled by the repercussions for Yingying. Against the obvious sympathy Yingying wins by the code of romance, Zhang has to justify his betrayal.

Now at last he can finish the poem "Meeting the Holy One." Verse renditions of romantic stories, both in quatrains and long ballads, were clearly very popular in the Mid-Tang, from Yang Guifei to Li Wa to dozens of other tales, including Yingying's own story. Prose narratives often give complicated and nuanced accounts of human behavior; for all its undeniable virtues, however, poetry flattens these complications out into purified roles. In his poem "The Song of Lasting Pain" 長恨歌 Bai Juyi does not tell us what the prose tale does, that in Yang Guifei the emperor Xuanzong had taken one of his son's concubines. Similarly in Yang Juyuan's quatrain on Yingying, the complications of the letter are reduced to "her broken heart."

Framed in this painfully human prose narrative, poetry comes off even worse than usual. In Yuan Zhen's "continuation" of Zhang's "Meeting the Holy One," the myth of the goddess' visitation is elaborated, followed by the inevitable separation and longing gaze, with fond regard for the lingering traces. We may note how their separation is "poetically" transformed:

方喜千年會，俄聞五夜窮。
留連時有恨，繾綣意難終。
慢臉含愁態，芳詞誓素衷。
贈環明運合，留結素心同。
啼粉流宵鏡，殘燈遠暗蟲。
華光猶苒苒，旭日漸瞳瞳。
乘鶩還歸洛，吹簫亦上嵩。
衣香猶染麝，枕膩尚殘紅。
幂幂臨塘草，飄飄思渚蓬。
素琴鳴怨鶴，清漢望歸鴻。
海闊誠難渡，天高不易沖。
行雲無處所，簫史在樓中。

No sooner made glad by this millennial
    meeting,
she suddenly heard night's hours end.
At that moment resentful, she lingered on,
clinging with passion, desire unspent.

A sad expression on languid cheeks,
in sweet lines she vowed the depths of love.
Her ring-gift revealed a union fated,
a love-knot left showed hearts were the same.
Cheeks' powder in tears flowed on night's
    mirror,
lamp's last flickering, insects far in the dark.
As the sparkling rays still dwindled away,
the sun at dawn grew gradually bright.

She rode her cygnet back to the Luo;
he played his pipes as he climbed Mount Song.
Her musk still imbued the scent of his clothes,
his pillow oily, still flecked with her rouge.

Thick grow the grasses beside the pool,
wind-tossed, the tumbleweed longs for the isle.
Her pale zither rings with the crane's lament,
she looks toward the stars for the swan's return.

The sea is so vast, truly hard to cross;
and the sky is high, not easy to reach.
Goddess moving in cloud, nowhere now to be
    found;
and Xiaoshi is there in his high chamber.[3]

Poetry removes the entire question of permanence in the relationship and any hint of choice in the lovers' separation. Poetry traps Zhang and Yingying in an archaic plot from which they cannot escape. In poetry their loves are perfectly equal. But the most remarkable transformation is found at the very end, in which Zhang is figured as the pipemaster, Xiaoshi, still awaiting his beloved, and Yingying is figured as the goddess, who deserts the man and disappears without a trace.[4]

There is such disparity between the prose account and the poetic transformation that we are led to wonder if it can be anything but ironic. There is evidence to suggest that Yuan

[3] Xiaoshi was the lover of the daughter of Duke Mu of Qin and went off to Heaven with her.

[4] It is also possible that Xiaoshi represents Yingying's husband.

Zhen is indeed the Zhang of the story, and yet we must wonder, both here and elsewhere, how this could be so. If Yuan Zhen is not Zhang, this is willful and ruthless irony; if Yuan Zhen is Zhang, it is "My Last Duchess" without irony.

"Every one of Zhang's friends who heard of the affair was stirred to amazement. Nevertheless Zhang had already made up his mind." That small word "nevertheless," *ran* 然, contains a wealth of otherwise suppressed information. It tells us that Zhang's friends thought he had done wrong, thought that he should marry Yingying. The public code of romance, so powerful in "Huo Xiaoyu's Story," is very much in force in the background. We see the presence of that suppressed judgment in Zhang's need to justify himself, to draw on powerful and persuasive arguments from the Chinese tradition about dangerous women that lead men to perdition. The response of Zhang's friends to such an argument is a deep sigh ("deeply moved"), *shentan* 深歎, perhaps suggesting assent, but assent of a peculiar kind. Clearly this potentially ambiguous response is not enough, for the narrator will not let go of the story until the public has given more explicit approval to Zhang's conduct.

Perhaps the only way to salvage Zhang's reputation is to bring Yingying out of the stasis of yearning and marry her off. This will effectively put an end to the romantic Huo Xiaoyu plot hanging over Zhang's head. Yingying had floridly written:

> But, perchance, the successful scholar holds love to be but of little account and sets it aside as a lesser thing in order to pursue things of greater importance, considering his previous mating to have been a vile action, his having taken enforced vows as something one may well betray. If this be so, then my form will melt away and my bones will dissolve, yet my glowing faith will not perish. My petals, borne by the wind and trailing in the dew, will still entrust themselves to the pure dust beneath your feet. Of my sincerity unto death, what words can say is all said here.

Against Yingying's eloquent protestations we read, "Somewhat more than a year later, Yingying married another, and

Zhang too took a wife." Yingying's marriage not only takes us out of the world of romance, it frames romance as a mere temporary aberration in a practical world.

Zhang passes by the place where Yingying is living with her husband, and he stops to visit her. Here again is one of those blind elisions that begs attention. After all that has occurred, why does he seek her out now that she is married? There is nothing innocent here: Zhang "asked her husband to speak to her, wanting to see her as a maternal cousin." By needing to be explicit about the grounds he used to see her—"as a maternal cousin," *yi waixiong* 以外兄—the narrator acknowledges that there is a problem and admits that if the husband knew the deeper and hidden basis of their relationship, he would never allow such a meeting to take place. When her husband innocently reports to Yingying that her cousin would like to see her and Yingying refuses, Zhang is offended! Yingying learns about this and in her weakness writes a quatrain, hinting that she still cares for him. Finally she writes the necessary quatrain releasing Zhang once and for all and removing the curse of Huo Xiaoyu from him:

還將舊時意，憐取眼前人。

Take what you felt in times gone by
and love well the person before your eyes.

At this point Zhang finally wins the public exoneration he sought: "People at the time generally accepted that Zhang was someone who knew how to amend his errant ways. At parties I have often brought up this notion. One would have those who know not do such things, but those that have done such things should not become carried away by them."

"Yingying's Story" is filled with interpretations, both interpretations that involve moral judgment, such as the final judgment of the male community reported above, and interpretations that transcend judgment, such as the romance of the goddess. From the middle of the story on, however, only the interpretations involving moral judgment remain in play. Zhang struggles desperately to put his "spin" on events, and whether or not we can identify Zhang with Yuan Zhen, there is no question that Zhang has a degree of control over the information that constitutes the story.

Why is it that modern readers, who are contented to take most Tang tales as inventions or elaborations of stories, are so interested in identifying the author of the tale with Zhang? Yuan Zhen, speaking as the author, takes special care to distinguish himself from Zhang: "I was on particularly good terms with Zhang and asked him to explain." The answer to the readerly impulse toward an autobiographical interpretation may be that the story is told so well that it ripples with a sense of vested interests. It is a troubling story, unlike anything else in the Tang. In contrast to invented stories or stories embellished from current gossip, this narrative never pretends to know what Yingying was thinking or what she did when outside Zhang's presence.

We can never know for certain whether Yuan Zhen was or was not the real Zhang. We cannot even know for certain if there really was a Zhang and a Yingying on whom the story was based (although we do know that the story was current at the time and was not invented by Yuan Zhen out of whole cloth). If Yuan Zhen was not Zhang, then he was a master of irony, holding opposing values in play and undermining them. This Yuan Zhen deserves a place beside Flaubert in his ruthless treatment of conventional morality and the fraudulent images of romance that ludicrously pretend to be alternatives to its oppressive sterility. If, however, Yuan Zhen was Zhang, then in trying to justify himself, he does not know what he is revealing. This second version is not unpersuasive: when trying too hard to make one case and suppress an alternative account, one may lend force to the very thing one least wants others to think. A person may actually be telling a very different story from the one he thinks he is telling. If we take Yuan Zhen as the Zhang of the story, then he tells us loudly how everyone agreed with him, that Yingying was a dangerous woman, a *youwu*, from whose clutches he was fortunate to escape. But we have no reason to feel any confidence in that claim if he still is so careful to distinguish himself from the fictional person to whom these events were supposed to have occurred: "I was on particularly good terms with Zhang and asked him to explain."

Supplementary Texts

❖

Supplementary Texts

Zhao Yi (1727–1814)
Poems on My Dwelling
in the Rear Park
(third of nine)

A visitor suddenly knocked at my door
with an offer of cash for some writing.
He asked me to do a tomb inscription
and insisted I make it flattering:
in political life, a Gong Sui or Huang Ba;
in learning, a Zheng or Zhu Xi.
I thought it would be amusing,
so I did just as he required.
I patched a piece of fine phrases together,
and, lo and behold, a true gentleman!
I checked this against what he really did,
it was hardly an ounce to my ten pounds.
Suppose what I wrote is handed down—
who could tell if the man was a fool or wise?
And perhaps they will cite it as evidence,
to be copied at last in historical tomes.
Now I see that in histories of old
the most part belongs to pure puffery.

Jiang Fang, "Huo Xiaoyu's Story"

During the Dali reign [766–79] one Mr. Li of Longxi, with the given name Yi, passed the *jinshi* examination. In the following year he was to take the higher examination, "Picking out the Finest," and was waiting to be put to the test by the Ministry of Personnel. He reached Chang'an in August of that summer and took a lodging in the Xinchang Quarter of the city. He was from an illustrious family and had shown real talent since childhood. At the time people said that his elegant phrases and splendid lines were unequaled, and well-established men who were his seniors were unanimous in acclaiming him. Whenever he thought with pride about his superior qualities, he longed to find a fair companion. He sought widely among the famous courtesans, but after a long time he still could discover no one suitable.

There was in Chang'an at the time one Miss Bao, a procuress, who had formerly been a maid of Commander-escort Xue. It had been more than a decade since she bought back her indenture contract and made a respectable marriage. With her ingratiating nature and clever tongue, she had contacts with all the powerful families and kinsmen of the imperial consorts, and she was commended as the best person around for quickness and savvy. Having constantly received good-faith commissions and rich presents from Li Yi, she was particularly well disposed toward him.

It happened that several months later Li Yi was idling away the time in the southern pavilion of his house. In the course of the afternoon, he suddenly heard an urgent knocking at his gate, which turned out to signal the arrival of Miss Bao. He hurriedly straightened his clothes to go greet her: "My dear Miss Bao, what brings you here so unexpectedly today?" Bao replied, "And has my young bookworm been having a pleasant dream? I have for you a fairy princess who has been banished to this lower world. She asks no money—she yearns only for a man of gallantry and feeling. Someone of this caliber is a perfect match for you." When Li Yi heard this, he leapt for joy and wonder. Drawing Bao by the hand, he bowed and expressed his gratitude, "I'll be your slave my whole life; I would die for you without flinching." Then he asked the girl's name and where she lived. Bao told him all the details. "She is the youngest daughter of the late Prince of Huo, Xiaoyu by name. The prince was extremely fond of her. Her mother's name is Jingchi, a maidservant who enjoyed the prince's favor. Soon after the prince passed away, Xiaoyu's brothers were not inclined to keep her in the household because she came from such a humble background; so they gave her a share of the wealth and sent her off to live elsewhere. She has changed her name to Zheng, and no one knows that she is the prince's daughter. In all my life I've never seen such a voluptuous figure. Yet she has noble sentiments and an independent manner. She surpasses others in every way. She understands everything from music to poetry and calligraphy. Recently she sent me to find her a good young man who is her equal in quality. I told her everything about you, and since she already knew of your name, she was exceptionally pleased and satisfied. She lives in Old Temple Lane in the Shengye Quarter, in the house just beyond the carriage gate. I've already set a date for you to meet— tomorrow at noon. Just go to the end of the lane and look for her maid Cinnamon, and you're there."

After Bao had left, Li Yi made his plans for the visit. He ordered his houseboy Qiuhong to go to his cousin, Lord Shang, the Capital Administrator, to borrow his fine black yearling and a golden bridle. He had his clothes laundered, and he bathed, taking special care to be well groomed. The combination of joy and excitement prevented him from sleeping the entire night. As daylight broke, he put on his turban and looked at himself in the mirror, afraid that she wouldn't find him to her liking. Then he paced back and forth until it was noon, at which point he rode with great haste directly to the Shengye Quarter. When at last he reached the place agreed upon, he saw a maid standing there waiting. She greeted him and asked, "Aren't you Li Yi?" He got down from his horse, and she led it next to the house, locking the gate securely behind her. He then saw Miss Bao coming out from inside. Still at a distance she laughed and said, "Now what brings you barging in here?" Li Yi continued joking with her as she led him in through a central gate. In the courtyard there were four cherry trees, and from the one in the north-west corner there was hung a cage with a parrot in it. When it saw Li Yi come in, it spoke, "A man is coming—quick, pull down the curtains!" By nature Li Yi was proper and reserved, and his heart was still apprehensive and beset by doubts. When he heard the bird speak out so suddenly, he was over-come with panic and didn't dare go on farther.

While he was still hesitating there, Miss Bao led Jingchi down the stairs to greet him. She invited him in, and they sat down across from one another. Jingchi was perhaps some-what over forty, delicate and still very attractive. She laughed and chatted and made herself agreeable. Then she said to Li Yi, "I had heard before that you are a man of both talent and feeling. Now I can see for myself the elegance of your appear-ance and bearing. This is clearly not a case when there's nothing behind a reputation. I have one daughter, and though she has been but poorly educated, her looks are not altogether ugly. It would be most fitting if she could make a match with a true gentleman. Miss Bao has discussed this idea with me often, so I will now order her to serve you re-spectfully as a wife." Li Yi thanked her, "I am a very ordinary and awkward person, of no particular distinction. I had not expected to receive such kind regard. If only you would con-descend to choose me for this, it would be a glory for me, alive or dead."

Then she ordered that wine and food be served and had Xiaoyu come out from her chamber on the eastern side of the hall. Li Yi went to greet her, but all he was aware of was something like an alabaster forest and jade trees throughout the whole room, casting their dazzling radiance back and forth, and as he turned his gaze, the crystalline rays struck him. Xiaoyu then went and sat by her mother, who said to her, "You are always fond of reciting:

> When I opened the curtains, wind stirred the
> bamboo,
> and I thought it was my old friend coming.

Those lines are from a poem by this very Li Yi. Better to see him in person than to spend the whole day imagining him as you recite." Xiaoyu lowered her head giggling and whispered softly, "But better still to hear of his reputation than to see him in person, for how could a man of talent be wanting in looks to match?" At once Li Yi rose and bowed saying, "The young lady loves talent; I value beauty. These two preferences here illuminate one another in a conjunction between talent and good looks." Mother and daughter looked around at one another smiling. Then they raised their wine cups in several rounds. Li Yi stood up and asked Xiaoyu to sing. At first she was unwilling, but her mother insisted. Her voice was bright and clear, and the handling of the melody was precise and wondrous.

When the drinking was finished, Miss Bao led Li Yi to the western wing to rest for the night. The courtyard was peaceful. and the chamber was a spacious one, with splendidly worked curtains. Miss Bao ordered the servants Cinnamon and Washed Gauze to help Li Yi take off his boots and undo his sash. A moment later Xiaoyu arrived. What she said to him was loving and tender, and the manner of her words was winsome. The instant she took off her gauze robes, he saw that her body was gorgeous. They lowered the bed curtains and drew close to one another on the pillows, experiencing the transports of pleasure. To Li Yi's mind even what happened on Wu Mountain and by the banks of the Luo could not have been better.[1]

---

[1] This refers to the legend of the goddess of Wu Mountain having a sexual encounter with the king of Chu in a dream.

In the middle of the night, Xiaoyu suddenly began to weep as she gazed on Li Yi: "I come from a courtesan background and know that I am not a proper match for you. Now, because of your love of beauty, I have been given to someone as kind and worthy as yourself. But I worry that one morning my beauty will be gone, and your love will leave and go elsewhere. Then the clinging vine will have nothing to cling to, and summer's fan will be cast away in the growing cool of the autumn. In the instant we were at pleasure's height, without realizing it sadness came." When Li Yi heard this, he could not help being stirred to sighs. Then he pillowed her head on his arm and said softly, "Today I have gained everything that I hoped for in this life. I swear never to abandon you, or may my body be torn to pieces and my bones ground to powder. My lady, how can you say such a thing? Please bring me a piece of white silk so I can write a vow on it." Xiaoyu then stopped weeping and ordered her servant Cherry to lift up the bed curtains and hold a candle, after which she gave Li Yi a brush and ink. Whenever she had moments to spare from practicing music, Xiaoyu had always liked poetry and calligraphy. The brush and inkstone brought from her chests had previously been from the prince's household. She then got out an embroidered bag from which she took three feet of white silk ruled with fine black lines, the type known as "Yue maiden." This she gave to Li Yi. Li Yi had always been quite talented, and no sooner did he take brush in hand than he had completed it, drawing metaphors of mountains and rivers, pointing to sun and moon as witnesses to his faith. Every line showed the utmost sincerity, and whoever heard it was much moved. When he finished writing, he ordered that it be put in a jeweled box. From then on they clung to one another like kingfishers in the paths through the clouds. They were together day and night like this for two years.

In the spring of the following year, Li Yi passed the higher examination, "Picking out the Finest," by his skills at calligraphy and composition, and he was given the post of Recorder of Zheng County. In June he had to go to take up his office, and he was supposed to also go to Luoyang to pay his respects to his parents. Most of his kinsmen and close friends in Chang'an went to the parting banquet. At the time there were still some remaining traces of spring, and the summer scenery was first coming into its glory. When the drinking was finished and the guests had gone their separate ways, thoughts of the coming separation twisted through their thoughts. Xiaoyu said to him, "Because of your reputation due to your talent and your family status, many people admire you. I am sure that quite a few will want to form a marriage connection with you. Moreover, you are in the position when, as they say, 'There are strict parents at home and no legitimate wife in your chamber.' Once you leave, it is inevitable that you are going to make an advantageous marriage. The words of the vow that you wrote were nothing more than empty talk. Nevertheless I do have one small wish that I want to put before you right now. Carry it forever in your heart. Will you hear me out?" Li Yi was shocked and amazed, "What have I done wrong to have you say something like this? Say what you have to say, and I will have to accept it." Xiaoyu then said, "I am eighteen now, and you are twenty-two. There are still eight more years until you reach that season of your prime when a man should establish a household. During this period I want to experience a lifetime of love and pleasure. After that it will still not be too late for you to make a fine choice from a noble family and conclude a marriage alliance. I will then cast the affairs of mortal men behind me, shave off my hair, and put on the black habit of a nun, and in doing so a long-standing wish will be fulfilled."

Li Yi was both touched and ashamed, and without realizing it his eyes were streaming with tears. He then said to Xiaoyu, "What I swore by the shining sun will be so until death. Even growing old together with you would not fully satisfy my intentions; so how could I have such a recklessly fickle heart? I beg you not to doubt me. Just live as usual and wait for me. By October I will surely have made it back to Huazhou. Then I will find someone to send to bring you to me. Our meeting is not that far away." In a few more days Li Yi said his final good-byes and went east.

Ten days after he reached his post, he asked for leave to go to Luoyang to see his parents. Even before he reached home, his mother had already worked out the arrangements to have him marry a Miss Lu, and the agreement had been settled. His mother had always been strict and unbending, and Li Yi wavered in indecision and did not dare refuse. In consequence he had to go to the bride's family to thank them according to custom, after which a close date was set for the wedding. The Lus were, moreover, a family of the highest rank, and when they married off one of their daughters, the value of the wedding gifts offered had to be set at a million cash. If anything less than this sum were offered, propriety demanded that they not proceed. Li Yi's family had always been poor, and the wedding required that he go looking for money. Using various pretexts he went far off to visit friends and relations, spending the period from autumn to summer traveling in the Yangzi and Huai River region. He had, of course, betrayed his vow and had gone long past the date set for his return. By silence and having her hear nothing from him, he wanted to put an end to Xiaoyu's hopes; and he charged his friends and relations in Chang'an not to let word leak out to her.

Ever since Li Yi had missed the appointed time for him to send for her, Xiaoyu had often sought news of him, but the various wild rumors and speculations were never the same from one day to the next. She went to consult soothsayers and tried all the various means by which fortunes could be told. For more than a year she kept her anxiety and her sense of outrage to herself. She lay wasting away in her empty chamber until she became seriously ill.

Despite the fact that Li Yi's letters had stopped altogether, Xiaoyu's hopes and fantasies did not leave her. She sent gifts off to friends and acquaintances in order to get them to pass on any news to her. In her desperation to get some word of him, all the savings on which she lived were used up. She would often give private instructions to the maids to secretly sell some ornament or piece of clothing from her trunks. Usually she would entrust these to Hou Jingxian's pawnshop in the Western Market to be put on sale. Once she instructed her maidservant Washed Gauze to take a hairpin of purple jade to have it sold at Hou Jingxian's establishment. On the street Washed Gauze met an old jade carver from the Imperial Craft Manufactories. When he saw what she was carrying, he came up and identified it, "That hairpin is a piece I myself made. When in years gone by the Prince of Huo's youngest daughter was going to have her hair put up into coils for her coming-of-age, he had me make this and gave me 10,000 cash in return. I have never forgotten it. Who are you, and how did you come by this?" Washed Gauze said, "My young mistress is that very daughter of the Prince of Huo. The household was dispersed, and she has fallen on hard times, having given herself to a man. A while ago her husband went off to Luoyang, and she has heard no news of him. It has been almost two years now, and she has become ill through her misery. She ordered me to sell this so that she could offer gifts to people and try to get some word of him."

The jade carver was moved to tears: "To think that the sons and daughters of the nobility could fall into such misfortune and end up like this! The years left to me will soon be done, and to see such reversals from splendor to decline is a pain not to be borne." He then led Washed Gauze to the mansion of the Princess Yanxian, where he recounted the whole story in detail. The princess too was deeply moved and gave her 120,000 cash.

At this time the daughter of the Lu family, to whom Li Yi was betrothed, was in Chang'an. Having completed his task of gathering together sums adequate for the marriage gifts, Li Yi returned to Zheng county. In the final month of that year, he once again asked for leave to go into the city. In secret he chose out-of-the-way lodgings and didn't let anyone know where he was. Li Yi had a cousin, one Cui Yunming, a graduate of the examination in the Confucian Classics. Cui had an extremely generous nature, and in years gone by he had always accompanied Li Yi at drinking parties at Xiaoyu's house. As they laughed and chatted over food and drink, he had never been treated with the least formal reserve. Whenever he had gotten a letter from Li Yi, he would always report it faithfully to Xiaoyu. And Xiaoyu for her part would always provide firewood, fodder, and clothing to help Cui out, so that Cui was especially grateful to her. When Li Yi arrived in Chang'an, Cui went and told Xiaoyu the entire truth. Xiaoyu then sighed in indignation, "How can such things happen in the world?" She then asked all her friends to use any means possible to get him to come to her.

Li Yi was aware that he had not kept the date he set with Xiaoyu and had betrayed his vow. He further knew of Xiaoyu's condition, that her sickness had made her an invalid. In his shame he hardened his heart against her and absolutely refused to go. He would go out in the morning and come home at night, trying in this way to avoid her. Xiaoyu meanwhile wept day and night and entirely forgot about eating and sleeping. She had hoped to see him at least once more, but finally there seemed to be no way. Her rage at the wrong he had done her deepened, and she lay sprawled helplessly on her bed. There were, of course, those in Chang'an who knew of her. Men of delicate feeling were uniformly moved by the strength of Xiaoyu's passion, while men of the more bold-hearted and impetuous sort were all enraged at Li Yi's casual heartlessness.

The season was May, and everyone was going on spring outings. Li Yi and five or six of his friends had gone to the Chongjing Temple to enjoy the peonies. They were walking along the western gallery, taking turns reciting lines of poetry. Wei Xiaqing, a native of the capital and intimate friend of Li Yi, was walking along with him in that company, and he said to Li Yi, "Today the weather and the scenery are splendid. All the trees and plants are in full flower. But think of poor Xiaoyu in her empty chamber, having to swallow the wrong done to her. The fact that you have been able to abandon her so absolutely shows that you are truly a hard-hearted person. A man's heart shouldn't be like this. You really ought to think about it!"

At the very moment he was criticizing Li Yi with such feeling, there suddenly appeared one of those bold-hearted and impetuous fellows, wearing light robes with a yellow satin shirt, carrying a bow under his arm. He was a handsome, dashing fellow, splendidly attired, with only one shaved-head Turkish servant in attendance on him. He had come up unseen and had listened to the conversation. All of a sudden he came forward and greeted him saying, "Aren't you Li Yi? My family comes originally from Shandong, and we are related by marriage to the kinsmen of the imperial consorts. Although I myself am lacking in the literary graces, I enjoy the company of worthy men. Having so admired your illustrious reputation, I have always longed to encounter you. What a fortunate meeting this is today that gives me the opportunity to cast eyes on your exquisite features! My own poor lodgings are not far from here, and I have there such musical entertainments as can provide pleasure to the heart. There are also eight or nine beguiling wenches and ten or so fine steeds, as you prefer. I would like you to stop by for a visit."

Li Yi's companions all listened to these words, and each in turn was moved by such eloquence. Thereupon they went riding off in the company of this bold-hearted gentleman. They wound their way swiftly through several quarters of the city until they came at last to the Shengye Quarter. Because they were getting closer to where Xiaoyu was staying, Li Yi lost his inclination to stop by for a visit, and inventing some excuse, he tried to turn his horse back. But the bold-hearted gentleman said, "My place is just a little farther. You're not going to back out on me, are you?" And with this he took hold of the reins of Li Yi's horse and led him along. Delaying in this fashion, they came at last to Xiaoyu's lane. Li Yi's spirit was in a daze; he whipped his horse trying to turn back. But the bold-hearted gentleman abruptly ordered several servants to hold him and force him to continue on. Moving swiftly, he pushed Li Yi in through the carriage gate and had it locked fast. He then announced, "Li Yi has arrived." The whole household was so startled with delight that their voices could be heard outside.

The night before Xiaoyu dreamed that a man in a yellow shirt had brought Li Yi to her, and when he reached the place to sit down, he had Xiaoyu take off her shoes. Xiaoyu woke with a start and told the dream to her mother, who explained, "Shoes come in pairs, like the pair formed when a man and wife are rejoined. To take them off is to come apart. Coming apart after being rejoined must mean the final farewell. From this I can tell that you will surely see him again, but after seeing him you will die."

At the break of dawn Xiaoyu asked her mother to comb her hair and do her makeup. Because Xiaoyu had been sick so long, her mother secretly thought that she was delirious and didn't believe her. Reluctantly she forced herself to comb Xiaoyu's hair and put on her makeup. But no sooner had she finished than Li Yi arrived. Xiaoyu had been bedridden for quite some time and needed another person's help even to turn over. But when she heard that Li Yi had come, she rose in a flash, changed her clothes, and went out, as if some divine force were moving her.

When she saw Li Yi, she held back her anger and gazed at him fixedly, saying nothing. Her wasted flesh and lovely features gave the impression that she could endure it no longer. For a moment she hid her face behind her sleeve, then looked back at Li Yi. Such things touch people painfully, and everyone present was sobbing. In a little while a few dozen dishes of food and jugs of wine were brought in from the outside. Everyone present was startled to see this, and they immediately asked where the food had come from. All of it had been sent by the bold-hearted gentleman in the yellow shirt. When the food and drink was laid out, they went to sit down.

Xiaoyu leaned to the side and turned her face, gazing sideways at Li Yi for a very long time. Then she raised a cup of wine and poured it out on the ground saying, "I am a woman; my unhappy fate is like this. You are a man; your faithless heart may be compared to this. Fair of face and in the flower of my youth, I perish swallowing my resentment. I have a loving mother at home, yet I will not be able to care for her. My fine silken clothes and the music of pipes and strings will from this point on be forever ended. I must carry my suffering to the underworld, and all of it was brought on by you. Li Yi, Li Yi! We must now say farewell for good. But after I die, I will become a vengeful ghost and allow you no peace with your wives and concubines for the rest of your days." With that she grasped Li Yi's arm with her left hand and threw the cup to the ground. With several long and mournful cries, she died. Her mother lifted the corpse and rested it in Li Yi's arms, telling him to call back her soul. But she did not revive.

Li Yi dressed himself in white mourning robes on her account and wept for her day and night with the deepest sorrow. Then, on the evening before she was to be buried, all of a sudden he saw her within the white-curtained spirit enclosure, her appearance as lovely and desirable as she used to be. She was wearing a pomegranate-colored skirt with a purple tunic and a red and green cape. She leaned against the curtain, took her embroidered sash in hand, and looking around at Li Yi said, "I am embarrassed to see that there is still such feeling in you that you have come like this to see me on my way. Even in the dark realms below I could not help being moved to sigh." Once she finished speaking, she was no longer to be seen. On the next day she was buried in the Yusu Plain near Chang'an. Li Yi came to her graveside and mourned until he could mourn no more, then turned back.

Somewhat more than a month later he carried out the wedding ceremonies with Miss Lu. Feelings of sadness and sympathy filled his heart, and he had no joy in it. In July of that summer, he went back to Zheng County together with his wife Lu. Ten days after he arrived, he was sleeping together with Lu when all of a sudden he heard the sound of someone calling outside the curtains. Li Yi woke with a start and looked: there was a man who seemed somewhat over twenty, with a graceful and handsome appearance, hiding behind the curtains and repeatedly calling to Lu. Li Yi rose frantically and went around the curtains several times, but all of a sudden the man was nowhere to be seen. From that point on he began to harbor evil suspicions in his heart and was jealous of everything. There were none of the easy pleasures of life between husband and wife. He had a close friend who reassured him, going over the affair in detail, and his mind gradually eased. But then again ten days later he was coming in from the outside as Lu was playing the zither on the couch. Suddenly he saw, tossed in from the gate, a box of variously colored ivory and gold filigree, a bit larger than an inch in diameter. This fell in Lu's lap. Around it was a piece of light silk tied in a love knot. When Li Yi opened it and looked inside there were two love beans, a scarab, a passion pill, and some aphrodisiac made from a foaling donkey. At that point Li Yi bellowed in rage, his voice like a tiger. He took the zither and beat his wife with it, questioning her to make her tell him the truth. But Lu could not explain any of it. After that he would often whip her violently and practiced every manner of cruelty on her, until at last he accused her publicly in open court and sent her away.

Once he had divorced Lu, Li Yi would sometimes share a bed with women of the lower classes, serving girls and concubines, but always he would grow jealous and suspicious. Sometimes he would find some reason and kill them. Li Yi once visited Guangling and there obtained a well-known young woman known as Miss Ying. Her appearance was sleek and seductive, and Li Yi was very pleased with her. Whenever they sat together, he would tell her, "In such and such a place I got such and such a girl, who committed such and such an offense, and I killed her in such and such a way." He would tell such stories daily, hoping in this way to make her frightened of him and keep his women's quarters free of sexual misconduct. When he would go out, he would take a washing tub and put it over Ying on the bed; then he would set seals all around it. When he got back he would check the seals all around, and only when he was satisfied would he break the seals and let her out. He also kept a very sharp sword and would say to his serving girls, "This is Ge Creek steel from Xinzhou, to be used especially for cutting off the heads of those who commit transgressions." Whatever woman Li Yi met, he would instantly become jealous. He married three times, and each of the others went like it did the first time.

Yuan Zhen, "Yingying's Story"

In the Zhenyuan reign [785–804] there was a certain man named Zhang, of a gentle nature and handsome appearance. He held steadfastly to his personal principles and refused to become involved in anything improper. Sometimes a group of friends would go off to a party and behave riotously. While the others tried to outdo one another in wanton and unbridled recklessness, Zhang would remain utterly composed, and they could never get him to act in an intemperate manner. At this time he was twenty-three and had never been intimate with a woman. When a close friend questioned him about this, Zhang excused himself, saying, "The famous lecher of antiquity, Deng Tuzi, was not a man of passionate desire; his were the actions of a brute. I am someone who is truly capable of passionate desire, but simply have not encountered it. How can I say this? Creatures of the most bewitching beauty never fail to leave a lasting impression on my heart, and this tells me that I am not one of those free of passion." And the one who had questioned him acknowledged this in him.

Not long afterward Zhang visited Puzhou. About a dozen leagues east of the city there was a residence for monks known as the Temple of Universal Salvation where Zhang took up lodgings. It happened that a widow, one Madame Cui, was on her way to Chang'an; and since her journey took her through Puzhou, she too stopped over at this temple. Madame Cui had been born a Zheng, and Zhang's mother had also been a Zheng. When they traced the family connection, it turned out that she was his maternal aunt at several removes.

That year Hun Zhen, the Military Governor, passed away in Puzhou, and Ding Wenya, the court officer left in charge, was not liked by the troops. After the funeral they rioted and pillaged widely in Puzhou. Madame Cui had a great wealth of household goods as well as many servants. The hostel was frantic with alarm, and they did not know where to turn for help. Zhang had earlier developed friendly relations with the circle around the commandant of Puzhou, and he asked for guards to protect Madame Cui. As a result no harm came to her. About a dozen days later the Investigator Du Que arrived with an imperial commission to take charge of the troops, and he issued commands to the army, after which the disturbance ceased.

Madame Cui was exceedingly grateful for Zhang's goodness, and she had a feast prepared in his honor. As they dined in the central hall, she said to Zhang, "Your widowed aunt lives on, carrying her young children with her. I have had the misfortune of a close call with a major outbreak of violence among the troops, and I truly could not have protected these children's lives. Thus it is as if my young son and daughter owe their lives to you. What you have done for us cannot be compared to an ordinary kindness. I would now insist that they greet you with all the courtesies due to an elder brother, in the hope that this might be a way to repay your kindness." Then she gave this order to her son. His name was Huanlang, a gentle and handsome boy somewhat over ten years old. Next she gave the order to her daughter: "Come out and pay your respects to your elder brother; you are alive because of him." A long time passed, and then she declined on the excuse that she wasn't feeling well. Madame Cui said angrily, "Mr. Zhang protected your life. Otherwise you would have been taken captive. How can you still keep such a wary distance from him!" After another long wait, the daughter came in. She wore everyday clothes and had a disheveled appearance, of not having dressed up specially for the occasion. Tresses from the coils of her hair hung down to her eyebrows and her two cheeks were suffused with rosy color. Her complexion was rare and alluring, with a glow that stirred a man. Zhang was startled as she paid him the proper courtesies. Then she sat down beside her mother. Since her mother had forced her to meet Zhang, she stared fixedly away in intense resentment, as if she couldn't bear it. When he asked her age, Madame Cui said, "From September 784, the first year of the emperor's reign, until the present year, 800, makes her seventeen years old." Zhang tried to draw her into conversation, but she wouldn't answer him.

Finally the party ended. Zhang was, of course, infatuated with her, and he wanted to express his feelings but had no way. The Cuis had a maidservant named Hongniang. Zhang greeted her courteously a number of times and then seized an opportunity to tell her what he felt. The maid was scandalized and fled in embarrassment, at which Zhang regretted what he had said. When the maid came the next day, Zhang was abashed and apologized, saying nothing more about what he wanted. But then the maid said to Zhang, "What you said is something you should not have dared to say and something you should not dare allow to get out. However, you know the kinship ties of the Cuis in some detail. Given the gratitude Madame Cui feels toward you, why don't you ask for her [daughter's] hand in marriage?" Zhang replied, "Ever since I was a child I have by nature avoided unseemly associations. When I have been around women, I would never even give them suggestive glances. I never would have thought that a time would come when I found myself so overwhelmed by desire. The other day at the party I could scarcely control myself. For the past few days I have walked without knowing where I am going and eaten without thinking of whether I am full or not. I'm afraid I won't last another day. If I had to employ a matchmaker to ask for her hand in marriage, with the sending of betrothal tokens and the making of formal inquiries about names, it would be another three months, and I would be a fish so long out of the water that you would have to look for me in a dried fish store. What do you think I should do?" The maid replied, "Miss Cui is virtuous and guards herself scrupulously. Even someone she held in the highest regard could not lead her into misconduct by improper words; plans laid by lesser folk will be even harder to carry through. She does, however, like to compose poems and is always mulling over passages, spending a long time on pieces of wronged love and admiration. You should try to seduce her by composing poems that express your love indirectly. Otherwise there will be no way."

Zhang was overjoyed and immediately composed two "spring verses" to give to her. That evening Hongniang came again and handed over a piece of colored notepaper to Zhang, saying, "Miss Cui has instructed me to give you this." The piece was entitled "The Bright Moon of the Fifteenth." It went:

> I await the moon on the western porch,
> my door half ajar, facing the breeze.
> Flower shadows stir, brushing the wall—
> I wonder if this is my lover coming.

Zhang understood the subtle message implied. That night was the fourteenth of April. There was an apricot tree on the eastern side of her apartments, and by climbing it he could get into her quarters. On the following evening, the fifteenth, when the moon was full, Zhang climbed the tree and got into her quarters. When he reached the western porch, the door was indeed half ajar. Hongniang was lying there asleep in her bed, and Zhang roused her. Hongniang was startled: "How did you get in here?" Zhang lied to her, "Yingying's note summoned me. Now go tell her that I'm here." Soon afterward Hongniang returned, saying over and over again "She's here! She's here!" Zhang was overjoyed and surprised, certain that he would succeed in this enterprise. But when Yingying did arrive, she was in proper attire with a stern expression on her face. She proceeded to take Zhang to task item by item: "By your kindness you saved our family, and that was indeed generous. For this reason my sweet mother entrusted you with the care of her young son and daughter. But how could you use this wicked maid to deliver such wanton verses to me! I first understood your saving us from molestation as virtue, but now you have taken advantage of that to make your own demands. How much difference is there between one form of molestation and the other? I had truly wanted to simply ignore your verses, but it would not have been right to condone such lechery in a person. I would have revealed them to my mother, but it would have been unlucky to so turn one's back on a person's kindness. I was going to have my maid give you a message, but I was afraid she would not correctly convey how I truly feel. Then I planned to use a short letter to set this out before you, but I was afraid you would take it ill. So I used those frivolous and coy verses to make you come here. Can you avoid feeling shame at such improper actions? I want most of all that you conduct yourself properly and not sink to the point where you molest people!" When she finished her speech, she whirled about and went off. Zhang stood there in a daze for a long time. Then he went back out the way he had come in, by that point having lost all hope.

A few nights later Zhang was sleeping alone by the balcony when all of a sudden someone woke him up. He rose in a flash, startled, and found that it was Hongniang, who had come carrying bedding and a pillow. She patted Zhang saying, "She's here! She's here! What are you doing sleeping!" Then she put the pillow and bedding beside his and left. Zhang rubbed his eyes and sat up straight for a long time, wondering whether he might not still be dreaming. Nevertheless, he assumed a respectful manner and waited for her. In a little while Hongniang reappeared, helping Yingying along. When she came in, she was charming in her shyness and melting with desire, not strong enough even to move her limbs. There was no more of the prim severity she had shown previously. The evening was the eighteenth of the month, and the crystalline rays of the moon slanting past his chamber cast a pale glow over half the bed. Zhang's head was spinning, and he wondered if she might not be one of those goddesses or fairy princesses, for he could not believe that she came from this mortal world. After a while the temple bell rang and day was about to break. Hongniang urged her to leave, but Yingying wept sweetly and clung to him until Hongniang again helped her away. She had not said a word the entire night.

Zhang got up as the daylight first brought colors to the scene, and he wondered to himself, "Could that have been a dream?" In the light there was nothing left but the sight of some makeup on his arm, her scent on his clothes, and the sparkles of her teardrops still glistening on the bedding. A dozen or so days later it seemed so remote that he was no longer sure. Zhang was composing a poem called "Meeting the Holy One" in sixty lines. He had not quite finished when Hongniang happened to come by. He then handed it to her to present to Yingying.

From that point on she allowed him to come to her. He would go out secretly at dawn and enter secretly in the evening. For almost a month they shared happiness in what had earlier been referred to as the "western porch." Zhang constantly asked about how Madame Zheng felt, and she would say, "I can't do anything about it." And she wanted him to proceed to regularize the relationship. Not long afterward Zhang was to go off to Chang'an, and before he went he consoled her by telling her of his love. Yingying seemed to raise no complaints, but the sad expression of reproach on her face was very moving. Two evenings before he was to travel, she refused to see him again.

Zhang subsequently went west to Chang'an. After several months he again visited Puzhou, and this time his meetings with Yingying lasted a series of months. Yingying was quite skilled at letter writing and a fine stylist. He repeatedly asked to see things she had written, but she would never show him anything. Even when Zhang repeatedly tried to prompt her by giving her things he himself had written, he still hardly ever got to look over anything of hers. In general whenever Yingying did show something to someone else, it was always the height of grace and polish, but she appeared unaware of it. Her speech was intelligent and well reasoned, yet she seldom wrote pieces in response to what he sent her. Although she treated Zhang with the greatest kindness, she still never picked up his verses in a poetic exchange. There were times when her melancholy voluptuousness took on a remoteness and abstraction, yet she continually seemed not to recognize this. At such times expressions of either joy or misery seldom showed on her face. On another occasion she was alone at night playing the zither, a melancholy and despairing melody. Zhang listened to her surreptitiously, for had he asked her to play, she would not have played any more. With this Zhang became even more infatuated with her.

Soon afterward Zhang had to again go west to Chang'an to be there in time for the literary examination. This time, on the evening before he was to leave, he said nothing of his feelings, but instead sighed sadly by Yingying's side. Yingying had already guessed that this was to be farewell. With a dignified expression and a calm voice, she said gently to Zhang, "It is quite proper that when a man seduces a woman, he finally abandons her. I don't dare protest. It was inevitable that having seduced me, you would end it—all this is by your grace. And with this our lifelong vows are indeed ended. Why be deeply troubled by this journey? Nevertheless, you have become unhappy, and there is no way I can ease your heart. You have always claimed that I am good at playing the zither, but I have always been so shy that I couldn't bring myself to play for you. Now that you are going to leave, I will fulfill this heartfelt wish of yours." Thereupon she brushed her fingers over the zither, playing the prelude to "Coats of Feathers, Rainbow Skirts." But after only a few notes, the sad notes became so unsettled by bitter pain that the melody could no longer be recognized. All present were sobbing, and Yingying abruptly stopped and threw down the zither, tears streaming down her face. She hurried back to her mother's house and did not come back.

The next morning at dawn Zhang set out. The following year, not having been successful in the literary competition, Zhang stayed in the capital. He then sent a letter to Yingying to set her mind to rest. The lines Yingying sent in reply are roughly recorded here:

I received what you sent, asking after me. The comforting love you show is all too deep. In the feelings between man

and woman joys and sorrows mingle. You were also kind to
send the box of flower cut-outs and the five inch stick of lip-
rouge—ornaments that will make my hair resplendent and
my lips shine. But though I receive such exceptional fondness from you, for whom will I now make myself beautiful?
Catching sight of these things increases my cares, and
nothing but sad sighs well within me. From your letter I am
given to understand that you are occupied by the pursuit of
your studies in the capital. The path to progress in studies
does indeed depend on not being disturbed. Yet I feel some
resentment that I, a person of so small account, have been
left behind forever in a far place. Such is fate. What more is
there to say?

Since last autumn I have been in a daze as though I did
not know where I was. In the chatter of merry gatherings I
sometimes make myself laugh and join in the conversation,
but when I am alone in the still of night, tears never fail to
fall. And when I come to dream, my thoughts usually are of
the misery of separation, which stirs me until I am choked
with sobbing. When we are twined together, absorbed in our
passion, for a brief while it is as it once used to be; but then,
before our secret encounter comes to its culmination, the
soul is startled awake and finds itself sundered from you.
Although half of the covers seem warm, yet my thoughts are
on someone far, far away.

Just yesterday you said good-bye, and now in but an instant the old year has been left behind. Chang'an is a place
of many amusements, which can catch a man's fancy and
draw his feelings. How fortunate I am that you have not forgotten me, negligible and secluded as I am, and that you
were not too weary of me to let me occupy your thoughts for
at least a moment. My humble intentions have no means to
repay this. But when it comes to my vow to love you forever,
that is steadfast and unwavering.

Long ago, connected to you as a cousin, I happened to be
together with you at a banquet. Having inveigled my maidservant, you consequently expressed your private feelings.
Young people are unable to maintain a firmness of heart.
You, sir, stirred me as [the Han poet] Sima Xiangru stirred
Zhuo Wenjun, by playing the zither. Yet I did not resist, as
did Xie Kun's neighbor by throwing down her shuttle when
he approached her. When I brought my bedding to your side,

your love and honor were deep. In the folly of my passion I thought that I would remain in your care forever. How could I have foreseen that, "once having seen my lord," it would be impossible to plight our troth. Since I suffer the shame of having offered myself to you, I may no longer serve you openly as a wife. This will be a source of bitter regret that will last until my dying day. I repress my sighs, for what more can be said? If by chance in the goodness of your heart you would condescend to fulfill my secret hope, then even if it were on the day of my death, it would be for me like being reborn. But, perchance, the successful scholar holds love to be but of little account and sets it aside as a lesser thing in order to pursue things of greater importance, considering his previous mating to have been a vile action, his having taken enforced vows as something one may well betray. If this be so, then my form will melt away and my bones will dissolve, yet my glowing faith with not perish. My petals, borne by the wind and trailing in the dew, will still entrust themselves to the pure dust beneath your feet. Of my sincerity unto death, what words can say is all said here. I sob over this paper and cannot fully express my love. Please, please, take care of yourself.

This jade ring is a thing that I have had about me since I was an infant. I send it to you to wear among the ornaments that hang at your waist. From the jade is to be drawn the lesson of what is firm and lustrous, thus unsullied. From the ring is to be drawn the lesson of what continues on forever, never breaking. Also I send a single strand of tangled silken floss and a tea-grinder of speckled bamboo. These several things are not valuable in themselves. My message is that I would have you, sir, be as pure as the jade, that my own poor aspirations are as unbroken as the ring, that my tear stains are on the bamboo, and that my melancholy sentiments are like this twisting and tangled thread. Through these things I convey what I feel, and will love you always. The heart is close, though our bodies are far. There is no time set for us to meet. Yet when secret ardor accumulates, spirits can join even across a thousand leagues. Please take care of yourself. The spring breeze is often sharp, and it would be a good idea to force yourself to eat more. Be careful of what you say and guard yourself. And do not long for me too intensely.

Zhang showed her letter to his friends, and as a result many people at the time heard of the affair. One good friend, Yang Juyuan, was fond of composing verses and wrote a quatrain entitled "Miss Cui":

> Pure luster of this young Pan Yue—
>   even the jade cannot compare;
> sweet clover grows in courtyard
>   as snows first melt away.
> The amorous young talent
>   is filled with spring desires—
> poor Miss Xiao, her broken heart
>   in a letter of just one page.

I, Yuan Zhen of Henan, completed Zhang's "Meeting the Holy One" in sixty lines.

> Pale moonlight breaks in above curtains,
> fireflies flash through the sapphire air.
> The distant skies begin to grow dim,
> and below, trees have grown leafy and full.
> Past the yard's bamboo come notes of dragon
>   flutes,
> the well-side beech is brushed by phoenix song.

> Her filmy gauze hangs like a thin haze,
> soft breezes resound with her waist-hung rings.
> Crimson standards follow the Goddess of the
>   West,
> the heart of clouds proffers the Lad of Jade.
> As night's hours deepen, people grow still,
> or meeting at dawn in the drizzling rain.
> Pearl-glow lights up her patterned shoes,
> blooms' brilliance hidden by embroidered
>   dragon.
> Jade hairpin, its colored phoenix in motion,
> gauze cape that covers red rainbows.
> He says that from this Jasper Flower Beach
> he must go to dawn court at Green Jade Palace.

> By his roaming north of the city of Luo
> he chanced on Song Yu's eastern neighbor.
> When he flirted, at first she gently refused,
> but in secret soft passions already conveyed.

From her lowered coils the tresses' shadows
    stirred,
her circling steps obscured in jade-white dust.
Face turned, glances flowed like flowers and
    snow,
she mounted the bed, bunched satins borne in
    arms.
Mated ducks, their necks twined in dance,
kingfishers encaged in passion's embrace.
Her black brows knit in modesty,
her carmine lips, warming, grew softer.
Breath pure as the fragrance of orchids,
her skin glossy, her marble flesh full.
Worn out, too tired to move her wrist,
so charming, she loved to curl up.
Her sweat flowed in beads, drop by drop,
her tangled tresses thick and black.

No sooner made glad by this millennial
    meeting,
she suddenly heard night's hours end.
At that moment resentful, she lingered on,
clinging with passion, desire unspent.
A sad expression on languid cheeks,
in sweet lines she vowed the depths of love.
Her ring-gift revealed a union fated,
a love-knot left showed hearts were the same.
Cheeks' powder in tears flowed on night's
    mirror,
lamp's last flickering, insects far in the dark.
As the sparkling rays still dwindled away,
the sun at dawn grew gradually bright.

She rode her cygnet back to the Luo;
he played his pipes as he climbed Mount Song.
Her musk still imbued the scent of his clothes,
his pillow oily, still flecked with her rouge.

Thick grow the grasses beside the pool,
wind-tossed, the tumbleweed longs for the isle.
Her pale zither rings with the crane's lament,
she looks toward the stars for the swan's return.

The sea is so vast, truly hard to cross;

and the sky is high, not easy to reach.
Goddess moving in cloud, nowhere now to be
found;
and Xiaoshi is there in his high chamber.

Every one of Zhang's friends who heard of the affair was
stirred to amazement. Nevertheless Zhang had already made
up his mind. I was on particularly good terms with Zhang
and asked him to explain. Zhang then said, "All such creatures ordained by Heaven to possess bewitching beauty will
inevitably cast a curse on others if they don't do the same to
themselves. Had Cui Yingying made a match with someone of
wealth and power, she would have taken advantage of those
charms that win favor from a man; and if she were not the
clouds and the rain of sexual pleasure, then she would have
been a serpent or a fierce dragon—I do not know what she
would have transformed into. Long ago King Shouxin of Yin
and King You of Zhou controlled domains that mustered a
million chariots, and their power was very great. Nevertheless, in both cases a woman destroyed them. Their hosts were
scattered, they themselves were slain, and even today their
ignominy has made them laughingstocks for all the world. My
own virtue is inadequate to triumph over such cursed wick-
edness, and for this reason I hardened my heart against her."
At the time all those present were deeply moved.

Somewhat more than a year later, Yingying married another, and Zhang too took a wife. He happened to pass
through the place where she was living and asked her husband to speak to her, wanting to see her as a maternal
cousin. Her husband did speak to her, but Yingying refused
to come out. The fact of Zhang's pain at such a rebuff showed
on his face. Yingying found out about this and secretly composed a piece whose verses went:

Ever since I have wasted to gauntness
and the glow of my face has gone,
I toss and turn thousands of times,
too weary to get out of bed.

> Not because of him at my side
>   that I am ashamed to rise—
> grown haggard on your account, I'd be
>   ashamed in front of you.

And she never did see him. A few days later Zhang was ready to go, and she composed another poem to say a final farewell.

> Rejected, what more can be said?—
>   yet you were my love back then.
> Take what you felt in times gone by
>   and love well the person before your eyes.

From that point on he knew nothing further of her.

People at the time generally accepted that Zhang was someone who knew how to amend his errant ways. At parties I have often brought up this notion. One would have those who know not do such things, but those that have done such things should not become carried away by them.

In a November in the Zhenyuan reign, my good friend Li Shen was staying over with me in the Jing'an Quarter. Our conversations touched on this affair, and Li Shen made particular comment on how remarkable it was. He consequently composed "Yingying's Song" to make it more widely known. Cui's childhood name was Yingying, and he used this in the title.

Index

Index

In this index an "f" after a number indicates a separate reference on the next page, and an "ff" indicates separate references on the next two pages. A continuous discussion over two or more pages is indicated by a span of page numbers, e.g., "57–59." Passim is used for a cluster of references in close but not necessarily consecutive sequence.

Library of Congress Cataloging-in-Publication Data

Owen, Stephen, 1946–
    The end of the Chinese 'Middle ages': essays in Mid-Tang literary culture /
Stephen Owen
        p.   cm.
    Includes index.
    ISBN 0-8047-2666-3 (alk. paper).   — ISBN 0-8047-2667-1 (pbk. : alk. paper)
    1. Chinese literature—T'ang dynasty, 618–907—History and
criticism.   2. Chinese poetry—T'ang dynasty, 618–907—History and criticism.
3. China—Intellectual life—221 B.C.–960 A.D.
I. Title.
PL2291.084   1996
895.1'109003—dc20   95-25619
                                                                                                    CIP

⊗ This book is printed on acid-free paper

Original printing 1996

Last figure below indicates year of this printing

05 04 03 02 01 00 99 98 97 96